KWEENS

HAPPINESS

DECODED

All in a pursuit to free women and empower change.

To all the extraordinary women out there, who courageously navigate the twists and turns of life's journey. May this book serve as a light, guiding you through some of today's complexities, whilst celebrating the wonders of womanhood. Your strength, resilience, and spirit inspire me every day.

Penny Dee

KWEENS - Happiness Decoded

First published in Great Britain in 2023 by Book Bubble Press.

A Borough Media Company

A CIP catalogue record for this title is available from the British Library.

ISBN: 978-1-912494-14-9

Also available in eBook ISBN: 978-1-912494-15-6

Author Website: www.pennydee.co.uk

Publisher Website: www.bookbubblepress.com

Contents

Introduction

Chapter 1: More to Life than Bliss?   1
Chapter 2: Hope Springs Maternal   21
Chapter 3: You've got to be Kidding!   45
Chapter 4: Men Earned, Women Spurned   71
Chapter 5: Happy Wife Happy Life   89
Chapter 6: The Change is Good   107
Chapter 7: Quackonomics   135
Chapter 8: Mic Drop   157

Acknowledgements   160
Book Index   162
Book Club   163
About the Author   166
Book Bonus   168

KWEENS

HAPPINESS
DECODED

for
Adult Human Females

Penny Dee

Book Bubble Press

United Kingdom

"Whose rules are you living by anyway? That's the question Penny Dee, businesswoman and Cheshire royalty, asks us to ponder in this mini-memoir, mini-manifesto.
Reading this as a woman of 'a certain age', I felt that Penny is definitely on my side, even (perhaps especially) when the rest of the world is not. It affirmed to me that, yes, I am a Queen, and from now on 'the Queen eats first!'"

Kerry Daynes - Forensic Psychologist, best selling author, campaigner and women's advocate.

Introduction

Join me on this fascinating journey as we delve into the depths of the female experience. Through this book, you will develop a profound understanding of the daily challenges faced by today's women—both the positive and negative aspects, as well as the bewildering moments.

It's time to break free from the chains that bind us and forge a new path where curiosity, self-reflection, and empowerment intertwine. With a laser focus on unravelling the thoughts and emotions that shape women's lives, we will fearlessly explore the pursuit of happiness from a female perspective. Uncovering uncomfortable yet empowering truths, this book shines a spotlight on the challenges women encounter whilst navigating a world suffused with societal expectations. My ultimate goal is to inspire readers to transcend these norms, carving out their own unique paths towards fulfilment. Throughout the book, I discuss highly controversial topics that significantly impact women's lives and their quest for happiness. Drawing from my own personal experiences and the stories shared by countless women I have encountered, I hope to trigger numerous "light bulb moments" that ignite transformative thinking. By unravelling the truth and dismantling the conditioning that women have endured, together we can embark on the ultimate journey of female empowerment.

By presenting an authentic perspective of the world as it truly exists, I implore you to liberate yourselves from the invisible shackles that have held you back. Embracing diverse viewpoints and challenging societal constructs is the key to shaping your own destinies, and paving the way for our fellow sisters.

I will share my own unique viewpoints and I invite you to join me on an immensely enjoyable adventure. Prepare to be enlightened, inspired, and empowered as we uncover the path to true happiness and self-discovery.

Decoded 1
Happiness

Chapter 1

MORE TO LIFE THAN BLISS?

In today's ever-evolving world, we find ourselves grappling with the concept of happiness and what it means to each of us. As we navigate the complexities of modern life, it becomes essential to examine what happiness really means for women in contemporary society, what it encompasses, and how it manifests in their unique experiences, aspirations, and challenges.

To understand happiness from a woman's perspective, we must consider the multifaceted aspects of her life. It goes beyond mere fleeting moments of joy or temporary satisfaction. Instead, it encompasses a holistic sense of fulfilment, purpose, and well-being that resonates across various domains.

For a woman today, happiness may entail finding fulfilment in professional endeavours, such as pursuing a career that aligns with her passions and values, breaking free from societal expectations and patriarchal norms, and being empowered to embrace her true potential. It could also involve nurturing meaningful connections, celebrating accomplishments, acknowledging the importance of emotional well-being by freely expressing her authentic self, transcending societal pressures and embracing her unique identity. Setting boundaries to prioritise her own well-being amidst the demands of daily life is also crucial.

In essence, defining happiness for a woman today is an individual and subjective journey. It is about shaping her own narrative, aspirations, and sense of purpose. It is acknowledging that happiness may look different for each woman and that her voice and experiences should be valued and heard.

As we strive for progress and inclusivity, it is crucial to create a world where women are empowered to pursue their version of happiness. By challenging societal norms, advocating for gender equality, and creating supportive environments, we can contribute to a future where women are not only permitted but encouraged to thrive on their own terms.

So, let us embark on this exploration of happiness by understanding that it is a deeply personal and ever-evolving journey for women today. I want to celebrate our resilience, amplify our voices, and work towards a world where our pursuit of happiness is not only simply accepted but wholeheartedly embraced for all.

As we reflect upon the past 45 years, it becomes evident that women's freedoms have undergone significant expansion. With the remarkable surge in educational attainment and the gradual reduction of the pay gap, among other achievements, women have undeniably made substantial strides. In general, we have made enormous gains, and with all of that opportunity comes more choice than ever.

However, data from NHS England in the UK shows that women are twice as likely to be prescribed antidepressants as men, with 5.5 million women prescribed the drugs in 2021/22 compared with 2.8 million men. These statistics raise questions about the societal factors contributing to the increasing reliance on these medications for women. Despite the gains and opportunities, women often find themselves caught in a confusing web of expectations in today's world. They are expected to have it all and do it all, but rarely do we stop to examine the pressures placed upon us from every direction.

It's time to shed light on the intricate complexities faced by women in the 21st century and address the need for balance and happiness. We must uncover the raw truths hidden beneath the contradictory and conflicting evidence. In our quest to understand what happiness really means for women, we must delve deeper and ask ourselves a fundamental question: *Are we truly in control of our own happiness, or is it dictated by external forces at every turn?* Take a moment to reflect on this. *Who holds the reins to your happiness? Is it you? Your family? Your work? Or something else?*

It's crucial to ponder these thoughts and examine the influence that various aspects of our lives exert on our well-being. The reality is that societal expectations, familial obligations, and professional demands often intertwine, creating a complex tapestry that can dictate our happiness if we allow it. As women, we must challenge norms and redefine our relationship with happiness. It's not a passive state to be granted or controlled by others. True happiness comes from taking ownership of our lives, setting boundaries, and pursuing our own passions and desires. It requires introspection and the courage to make choices that align with our authentic selves.

I want to shine a light on the truth and navigate the intricate paths that lead to happiness. By acknowledging the complexities we face and taking control of our own happiness, we can reshape our lives and create a more fulfilling and balanced existence. It's time to break free from the constraints imposed upon us and pave the way for a new narrative, one that empowers women to embrace their happiness on their own terms.

Is it the pressure to conform to unrealistic standards, the juggling act of multiple roles, or the perpetual struggle for balance in a demanding world? Could another contributing factor be the insidious erosion of women's rights from certain quarters in more recent years, causing us to question our own innate female instincts and shaking our foundations to their core? Delving into these complex issues sheds light on the unique challenges faced by women and prompts us to question the systems and structures that shape not only our world today but also our mental well-being.

Are we in control of our own happiness, or is our happiness controlled at every level? Have you ever asked yourself that question?

We live in a world where we are bombarded day and night, often unaware of the influence that surrounds us. We are constantly fed a diet of wants and desires through advertising and marketing, being subtly brainwashed and sold to at every turn. Ideas on how we should live our lives are imposed upon us every second of every day through various mediums such as social media, phones, computers, TV, music, retailers, governments, emails. The list goes on. So, how can we truly know if our dreams, desires, goals, and ways of living are genuinely what we want and will make us happy? What if we are unconsciously living our lives the way we are being told to? Perhaps, we are being constantly fed a stream of marketing messages, consciously and subconsciously, that directly impact our everyday decisions, whether we are aware of it or not.

In today's fast-paced world, our attention is constantly pulled in multiple directions, with an ever-growing demand from our devices. These devices have become constant companions, surpassing even our closest family members or beloved pets in the amount of time and attention we give them. They accompany us from the moment we wake to the time we rest our heads on the pillow at night, seamlessly integrating into every aspect of our lives. They keep us entertained, informed, and connected throughout the day and into the late hours of the night. Our devices have become intertwined with our existence, capturing our attention and shaping our experiences in ways we may not fully comprehend. Each notification vies for our immediate action, eventually eroding our attention span. It can become an assault on our senses. While I support progress and technology, what seems to be missing is the acceptance that these things should not dominate us. If we make them our masters, then who do we truly answer to? Ourselves or have we all become mere products?

Pondering the intricate dynamics of our modern existence, one cannot help but draw parallels to the popular late 90s film, The Matrix. It compels us to question whether we have become mere products of a system or if we are still autonomous beings. The iconic depiction of humans as batteries in the Matrix, powering a simulated reality, evokes a profound contemplation of our own place in the world. In this reflection, have we, in our relentless pursuit of progress and convenience, unwittingly succumbed to the role of commodities? Have we become cogs in a grand machine, serving the interests of a system that seeks to harness our attention for its own gain?

To give you an example of this in our everyday life, let's take a look at just one instance: advertisements online. Over the years, I've pondered the concept of customised ads. Having products of interest presented to us can be great on one hand, but on the other hand, we must consider whether cleverly placed advertisements create an artificial void that triggers FOMO (fear of missing out). I witnessed the sheer power of marketing firsthand within my clinical business, DPC Clinic, a popular haven for cosmetic and medical tattooing, skin treatments, and aesthetic services. Many times, particularly in the early days, clients would confide in me that they felt as if the universe was aligning when they found us. When they were contemplating getting their eyebrows tattooed, almost miraculously, our advertisement would appear like a cosmic invitation, prompting them to take the step and secure their appointment with us. This was a time when the term 'algorithms' had yet to permeate the collective consciousness of social media. Initially, I wondered if serendipity was at play, but after a while, it slowly dawned on me that it was not fate that brought them to us, and it didn't take long for me to comprehend the profound influence of those early Facebook advertisements.

In the hustle and bustle of our daily lives, it's all too easy to fall into the trap of forgetting that what we experience is merely a fleeting satisfaction, a temporary fix that falsely promises happiness. Our diminishing attention spans can further contribute to this predicament, leaving us in a state of perpetual confusion. It is in these moments that we are most vulnerable, susceptible to being caught off guard by the allure of immediate gratification. Are our desires and aspirations truly our own, or have they been shaped and moulded by a culture of consumerism and conformity? In our quest for success and societal acceptance, do we unknowingly perpetuate this cycle?

Yet, amidst these existential quandaries, we must also acknowledge the inherent resilience of the human spirit. Just as Neo, the protagonist of 'The Matrix,' transcended the confines of the simulated reality, we too possess the capacity for awakening and self-discovery. We have the ability to challenge the narratives that seek to confine us, to question the systems that attempt to subdue our individuality, and resist the allure of conformity and the temptation to be reduced to mere batteries. By taking responsibility and shaping our own narratives, we can break free from the shackles and embark on a path of true self-determination.

This brings me again to the eternal question: *What actually is happiness?*

Understanding its essence is crucial in order to find or cultivate our own happiness. As someone with an interest in behavioural psychology and studying it further in college, as well as the cellular intricacies of the brain, I find myself drawn to questions that delve deeper. One such question revolves around the concept of our existence as intricate supercomputers, programmed to think and feel in predetermined ways. Could it be that we are susceptible to manipulation, unknowingly embracing ideas or narratives that conveniently align with hidden motives, all the while suppressing our innate intuition?

The constant influx of external influences, whether through social or mainstream media, social interactions, or societal expectations, can sway our perceptions, making us susceptible to subtle manipulations that shape our thoughts, beliefs, behaviours, and decisions. As I embark on my own journey of self-development, I find myself caught between the desire for genuine self-expression and understanding the impact of external influences on my own thoughts and actions. Yet, despite these challenges, I remain steadfast in my pursuit of self-discovery and the quest for an authentic understanding of happiness. I strive to discern the subtle nuances of my own thoughts and feelings amidst the distracting external voices. By honing our awareness and embracing critical thinking, we can navigate through the maze of manipulation and cultivate a sense of genuine selfhood.

Despite the attempts to shape and mould our thoughts and emotions, I firmly believe that we possess the innate power to challenge, question, and rise above these external influences. By continually questioning the narratives presented to us and cultivating a deep connection with our inner selves, we can free our thoughts, and in doing so, uncover our own genuine happiness that resonates deeply within us all.

We do know that happiness is about the journey. If you look at Buddhists and other spiritual beliefs, they state that once you actually reach 'your enlightenment,' it's all over for you in this particular life. You are then free to move on to the next level, which is, incidentally, unknown. For me, thinking of life as a journey gives me balance and perspective. I understand that it's about the experiences and relationships we have with humans, animals, and nature, and how we learn from them along the way. The greatest joy comes from those moments of clarity, where you tackle the next lesson with grace, realising that you have had previous life experiences that relate back to the current situation you find yourself in. When that familiar sense of understanding arises in the face of life's challenges, you can apply your hard-gained knowledge or wisdom to make things go smoother this time. It feels great, like that piece of the jigsaw slotting in. If we can survive the downfall, it's how we get up, move forward, and grow that counts, and more importantly, how we learn from it to progress on our journey.

Do you have a friend who keeps experiencing the same negative situations, whether it's a job that keeps going wrong or relationships where she repeatedly chooses inappropriate partners? Perhaps that friend is you. I believe many of us have been in that position. As I reflect on these situations, I've noticed that as I grow older, it becomes clearer that if I acknowledge my mistakes, learn from them, and move on, I generally don't encounter the same lesson again. I've also observed this process in others. When ownership of the situation isn't taken, it intensifies its demand for our attention until the lesson is learned from that particular challenge. This repetition will continue until responsibility is finally embraced. Only by taking true responsibility, acknowledging the impact of our own actions on our outcomes, and learning the lesson, can we progress. Moreover, as we incorporate that experiential knowledge into our lives, we can truly move forward.

Sometimes we can't control the circumstances that occur in our lives, but we always have the power to choose how we respond to them. It's essential to remember and emphasise this point: *We cannot control everything that happens to us in life, but we can control how we react to it.*

Often, our suffering arises not from the events themselves, but from our reactions to them. You may think that this discussion is veering towards spirituality, and that might not be your area of interest. However, I urge you to stay with me, as this book aims to open your eyes and hearts to our lives and the world around us. Could this act of opening ourselves up be a form of spirituality in itself, considering that being present in the moment is one definition of spirituality? What does spirituality mean to you? Some people associate it solely with organised religion, which may not resonate with everyone. It is helpful, however, to understand the distinction between religion and spirituality. Is spirituality about finding meaning and purpose in the things we value? Is it the search for inner peace, well-being, and tranquillity of the mind? Is it living in a state of contentment and happiness, having a sense of belonging, and cultivating loving relationships with ourselves and others? Regardless of your perspective, the important point is that we need to understand where our happiness will come from, but we cannot find it until we know what we are seeking. Spiritualism appears to be a guiding source that provides answers.

Budhist believe that true happiness lies within us all if we can just let it go. When we detach ourselves from our emotions and from specific outcomes. It involves cultivating the understanding that genuine peace and contentment come from focusing our time and energy on things within our control, while gracefully letting go of those things that are beyond our influence.

The Serenity Prayer articulates this beautifully: "Grant me the serenity to accept the things I cannot change, the courage to change the things I can, and the wisdom to know the difference."

By embracing this profound wisdom, we free ourselves from the burdens of attachment and expectations, allowing inner peace to flourish within us. This shift in perspective, achieved through detachment, enables us to embrace each moment as it arises and to let go with serenity.

Detachment can indeed play a significant role in finding true happiness. The idea of detachment, as advocated by Stoic philosophy and other wisdom traditions, involves recognising the distinction between what is within our control and what is not. By focusing our energy on the things we can influence and letting go of the things beyond our control, we can free ourselves from the unnecessary attachments and expectations.

Taking back control of our thoughts is a key aspect of reclaiming our happiness. Our thoughts shape our perception of the world, our emotional experiences, and our actions. By cultivating awareness and actively directing our thoughts towards more positive and empowering perspectives, we can change how we interpret and respond to life's events.

Stoic philosophy emphasises the importance of understanding the principle that some things are within our control, while others are not. This recognition forms the foundation for finding happiness and freedom. By accepting the limits of our control and directing our efforts towards what we can influence — such as our thoughts, attitudes, and actions — we can navigate life with greater clarity, resilience, and peace of mind.

Famous Stoic philosophers like Marcus Aurelius, Seneca, and Epictetus have explored these principles extensively. Epictetus, for instance, highlighted the connection between happiness and understanding what is within our control. By recognising this distinction, we can focus our attention and efforts on the aspects of life that we can actively shape and influence.

Derren Brown, a modern-day Stoic, delves into the subject of happiness in his book aptly titled *"Happy."* Exploring Stoic principles and other insights, he offers perspectives and practical guidance on finding happiness in our lives. It is a book that I thoroughly enjoyed, have read several times, and actually recommend that everyone should read. There are many great resources available on Stoic philosophy, mindfulness, positive psychology, and personal development. Consulting books, articles, and other materials can provide additional perspectives and insights to support your journey towards happiness and self-discovery and I have included some book recommendations at the back of this book for you to explore.

Personally, I find that when I detach from something, I can take a wider, higher view of it. I find it incredibly empowering when I understand that I'm no longer a slave to what I think I should think or feel. Instead of my actions being driven by unchecked emotions, I apply a mixture of logic and intuition to come to a conclusion and create a plan forward.

Have you ever stopped and thought about the type of person you are when it comes to decision making and taking action? Are you the kind of person who enjoys making impulsive decisions without much thought, or are you a meticulous planner who thrives on mapping out every intricate detail? Perhaps you're someone who ponders and reflects, allowing your intuition to guide you towards a well-timed plan, unfolding precisely when needed. If you want to delve deeper into your personality type, a useful tool to start with is the Myer Briggs personality type.

In my earlier career days when I was in the heady world of Information Technology corporate sales, I used to leave proposals to the last minute because I could feel that my brain needed that bit of pressure to bring out the greatness. It was like it seemed to fire in a slightly different way, as the extra pressure formed new neural pathways, and ultimately, the solution would always present itself to me. Even now, if I explore various solutions, taking ideas to their finite ends, I discover the answer for certain situations. I often marvel at how obvious that solution was and wonder why I didn't think of it in the first place. But as I grow older, I understand that, for me, I have to embrace that often pressurised brain process.

In this book, I want to take you on a journey that will help get you closer to your happiness. Being a woman today has never been more confusing. We are told we never had it so good: we have contraception, careers, bank accounts, mortgages, children, and choice... or do we? The issue is, I'm not convinced that the playing field is as level as we have been led to believe.

I am going to delve into some carefully and purposely chosen topics, pose questions, and challenge ideas that have gone unchecked for years, enabling you to see things from a whole new perspective and awaken your awareness. In my opinion, once we have awareness of these things, we can start making some changes and challenge that status quo.

You'll discover some outrageous injustices and inequalities that persist even today, and they may be things we blindly ignore in our everyday lives. We are so desensitised to these norms that we can't even pinpoint where these bizarre 'life rules' that we live by (more on those life rules later) even came from originally. Rules which were not actually designed for us to thrive, although we aren't supposed to know that. I'll shine some light; it'll be controversial, funny, enlightening, and my hope is utterly empowering. I hope you find that this book will hold profound revelations about your happiness, where it comes from, and how you can improve it. Once you know the truth about what women are thinking and feeling, I hope female empowerment ripples out and that I alter your perception of the world we live in today forever. With this newfound knowledge, you will have the keys to reclaiming your power and happiness.

Join me on this exhilarating journey that awaits in the chapters that lie ahead, unearthing the secrets that will help you pave the way to your ultimate joy and fulfilment. Knowledge is power, but I have to warn you, you may not look at life the same way again. In fact, I GUARANTEE you won't look at life the same again, and it will all be for the better. Welcome to my world!

Decoded 2
Mothers

Chapter 2

HOPE SPRINGS MATERNAL

Let's dive straight into the deep end and tackle a BIG topic: maternal relationships! Are you ready for a dose of controversy mixed with eye-opening revelations? This is thought-provoking, and it may challenge your perspectives, but trust me, it's worth exploring.

When we think about our happiness, we often consider our day-to-day lives, our work, environment, comfort, financial status and more. One of the main indicators of happiness has been shown to come from our relationships. This includes our immediate family and friends, as well as our involvement in our communities.

In this chapter, we will explore relationships with our mothers, and I think it's fair to say that I don't get on particularly well with mine.

One of the magical aspects of self-care is the bond between you and your Skin Therapist. The discrete nature of our work means that I hear about these amazing women's lives in unguarded moments, which provides true insight into what women think and feel. It's one of the joys of my clinical work and what you will read about as we delve further.

One of the subjects that frequently arises is family relationships, specifically the relationship between mother and daughter. I find it fascinating that many women only feel comfortable opening up once they know they are in understanding company. Once it becomes clear that I genuinely understand and I am there to listen without judgement, they always open up. It's as if their strained relationship with their mother is the final taboo.

It's a pleasant surprise when I occasionally hear that a daughter has no problem dedicating a good chunk of her precious time each week to her mother's needs. They tell me about how much of their schedule is devoted to doing things for their mum, and when I ask if they are okay with that, some express genuine happiness in doing so. They explain that their mum has always been there for them, that they love and adore her, and that she has been an amazing mother. It's a refreshing perspective that I don't hear that often. Usually I hear the phrase 'well, she's my mum,' which speaks volumes without saying much. If I probe further, I notice a slight crack in the veneer. Often, I only discover the full extent of the horror in that maternal relationship as I get to know the individual better, usually during our third or fourth appointment, when I mention that I don't speak to my own mother and pick up on some tension surrounding this topic. That's when stories of appalling cruelty and excessive demands start to emerge. But I can see their sheer fear of being judged when admitting that their mothers are vile. Or perhaps it's simply a matter of not considering it the 'right thing' to criticise a parent.

Why is it that so many intelligent, kind, caring, thoughtful, funny, adult women allow their mothers to talk to them as if they are insignificant? They endure derision, belittlement, and quite extraordinary levels of cruelty or hurtful remarks. In any other relationship, we would treat someone who treats us poorly accordingly — either by cutting them out of our lives or at the very least restricting our time with them and pushing back against their excessive demands. However, this rule of thumb doesn't seem to apply when it comes to family.

With friendships and personal relationships, we typically seek a foundation of mutual respect and admiration. We choose to spend our precious time with those who love, like, and appreciate us. Despite this, 'family' seems to bypass these social norms. In my own experience, I reached a point where I thought to myself, 'I wouldn't even speak to my worst enemy the way I am being spoken to and treated by my own mother.'

I vividly remember a phone conversation with my mother, discussing my upcoming wedding to my now-husband, Phil. Although I had never envisioned myself as a traditional white-dress bride, I had found a dress with a Greek goddess vibe that I loved. I excitedly shared this with my mother, expecting her to be pleased that I had found my dress so easily. Instead, I could hear the confusion and venom in her voice as she asked about the size I had bought. I told her I had purchased a UK size 16. She proceeded to question my decision, suggesting that I should strive to lose a significant amount of weight before the big day. She couldn't fathom the idea that I might dare to believe I could look beautiful or even acceptable at 'that size' on my wedding day. In response, I explained that when Phil had commented that he thought I would look gorgeous in a white dress, he meant me as I am, not some artificially slimmed-down version of me.

I've never quite understood why many women feel the need to lose substantial amounts of weight for their weddings. While I understand wanting to tone up and enhance the appearance of a dress and feel your absolute best on your big day, I've always believed that the person you are marrying should love and accept you for who you are, not some dramatically altered version of you — especially if you have never been that particular target weight before.

After the escalation of my mother's barbed remarks and, frankly, plain nastiness aimed at me, I asked her why she thought it was appropriate to talk to me, her daughter, like that. Her response was to tell me how Claire Balding, the BBC presenter, had finally lost "all of her weight" after her mother had called her out on it. Did my mother (who had been overweight and, yes, fat her whole life) seriously think this was an expression of motherly love? In her own twisted world, she probably did. However, in my world, I believed that a mother should be supportive and speak with kindness. With that thought, I flatly told her she wasn't welcome at our wedding, hung up the phone, and cancelled her hotel room. I was done with her. It was the final straw that broke the camel's back. This particular exchange is one that sticks in my mind, but I could probably write a whole book, indeed a full series of books, about it. However, I do know that this example is relatively tame in comparison to some of the stories I've heard.

When I first met Phil and knew our relationship was serious, I knew that I would have to arrange that first meeting with my parents. So, I did the obligatory briefing with him about my family, and more specifically, my mother. I did my best not to scare him off but to warn him not to take any hostility or odd remarks to heart and concluded by telling him, "That's just how she is." It was only when we were chatting over wine a few days after that first meeting that he revealed I had massively underplayed how nasty my mother was! At that point, we had only been together for a couple of months, and he was still navigating our family dynamics for himself. The matter-of-fact, subtle way he dropped that information into the conversation was appreciated. He knew it was a gamble, but his honesty and understanding showed me that he truly was the man for me. Phil, who possesses wonderful, quiet, self-assured confidence, and is honest and kind, was genuinely appalled by her behaviour that night. I'm sure she believed she was charming, while I had likely become somewhat desensitised to her at that point. In fact, I can't even recall a particular incident from that night, which demonstrates how we can tolerate bad behaviour from our loved ones, like the slow drip of water wearing us down.

Quite a few years ago, I met a woman at my clinic whom I immediately liked. It was evident that she possessed a lovely, kind-hearted disposition. During our usual chit-chat, our conversation turned to the topic of mothers. This particular lady confided in me that she felt a tremendous sense of relief to have someone to talk to about her situation. In her circle of friends, she found that no one else seemed to have a dysfunctional relationship with their mother. Whenever she broached the subject over the years, she didn't receive the support she had hoped for. This left her feeling even more isolated, with a hint of hostility. It seemed as though speaking ill of one's mother was strictly forbidden, regardless of one's true feelings towards her. Reflecting on the lack of empathy this woman had experienced from her friends, I realised that while sympathy may not always come easily, empathy should be more within reach for your close friends. I got the impression that this lady was very giving with her time and energy. Unfortunately, what she shared next was quite distressing. It became evident that her mother displayed clear narcissistic tendencies, manipulating and turning the rest of the family against her for no apparent reason. The cruelty she endured went beyond imagination. It left her with a deep-seated well of hurt and resentment. She questioned why her brother had been favoured over her and why her mother constantly criticised her, among other things. She even wondered if her mother resented her due to being her father's favourite.

However, regardless of the underlying reasons, it certainly didn't excuse the behaviour she had endured.

When your mother constantly belittles, excludes, and personally attacks you, it's natural for self-doubt to creep in. These situations have a powerful effect. The attacker knows that their words will hit home, causing you to question yourself and alter your behaviour. They rely on this to make you doubt yourself. From there, the manipulation intensifies, gradually eroding your self-worth. Seeking their approval becomes vital, even though it is rarely granted. If you try to distance yourself and think independently, they escalate their tactics. Being subjected to unrelenting personal remarks that breeds a sense of helplessness. Their continuous mockery leaves you feeling isolated. Outwardly, the narcissist may appear lovely, charming, and charismatic, successfully fooling others; however this is classic "gaslighting" or emotional manipulation. Regardless of the term used, its impact can be hugely detrimental and affect your entire life. It's no wonder that those who have experienced it feel alone and isolated. It can also initiate a cycle of people-pleasing on a broader level, as individuals attempt to gain approval from their mother or the person manipulating them.

You may have come across the term "gaslighting" before, but perhaps you haven't fully understood its meaning or how and why it has become a common phrase in recent years, particularly in the context of romantic relationships. When I reflect on my own family, the truth is that my mother and other immediate family members had been attempting to gaslight me for many years, if not my entire life.

Interestingly, the term "gaslighting" originates from a 1938 British play called "Gas Light," in which a deceitful husband uses lies and manipulative techniques to isolate his wealthy wife, making her doubt her own sanity so he could steal from her. In the play, whenever he exhibits this behaviour, the gas lights in the house flicker. It's worth noting that the term itself is never actually used in the play or subsequent film adaptations made shortly afterward. It wasn't until recently that the term gained popularity and became widely used in common language.

The real mystery is how I managed to maintain my sense of self and self-confidence despite the constant stream of passive-aggressive and sometimes not-so-passive words that were often directed at me. Fortunately, I would say it hasn't left any lasting damage, but perhaps my psychotherapist will be the judge of that in the future! All jokes aside, detangling myself from my immediate family for good wasn't an easy process at the time, but I can confidently say it was the best decision I ever made.

A few years later, I ran into the same woman previously mentioned, and she shared with me the news that her mother had passed away. Curious about her feelings on the matter, I asked how she had been affected by it. She replied that she felt somewhat numb. She had come to accept that nothing she could ever do or say would appease her mother. Despite giving her mother multiple chances to mend their relationship, she had learned the hard way that it's impossible to win with these types of people. Even in death, her mother had made one last cruel demand. When she asked if she could attend the funeral, she was told that she could, but with the strict condition that she could not bring her husband or her own family as this was the expressed wishes of the deceased. It's worth noting that her husband and her mother had never had any conflicts or disagreements; this demand was solely meant to strip away any support her daughter might have had in that hostile yet emotionally charged environment. Fortunately, she made the decision not to attend, which served as a final act of rebellion against her mother's controlling behaviour.

If you suspect there is a narcissist in your circle, be attentive to these classic narcissistic lines:

- "I am only saying it because I love you" or similar phrases.
- "You're being dramatic."
- "That's a silly idea."
- "You are a horrible/difficult girl."
- "You're being too sensitive or imagining things."

This is just a sample list, and there are many more manipulative phrases that narcissists may use. The purpose behind these statements is to belittle, confuse, hurt, and damage you, as they strive to exert control over you.

There is also another dimension to this which needs bringing to light and that is where mothers show favouritism towards their sons while treating their daughters differently. It's not uncommon for women to feel that their brothers receive an excessive amount of love and attention. This unequal treatment further accentuates the absence of love and affection that daughters experience. When a woman observes the contrasting attitudes and dynamics between her mother and her brother, she may come face to face with internalised misogyny for the first time. The blatant favouritism shown to her male sibling and the differential treatment she receives can unknowingly shape her perception of gender dynamics. These subtle messages can become deeply ingrained and hidden, only to surface when she realises that she has internalised the belief that men should come before her. This realisation can be the starting point for people-pleasing tendencies or self-esteem issues. For instance, if growing up, the sons were not expected to do household chores while the daughters were, or if the boys were given more freedom and financial privileges without conditions compared to their sisters. These gender disparities continue into adulthood, with the daughters still enduring belittling, criticism, demands, and being taken for granted by their dominant mothers, while their brothers are seen as flawless angels.

It's important to recognise these patterns and work towards dismantling them, promoting equal treatment and fostering healthy relationships within the family. Every individual deserves love, respect, and fairness, regardless of their sex.

In addition to the phenomenon of favouring sons, there is an additional burden placed on women known as the "sandwich generation." This particular group finds themselves managing not only their own children, household responsibilities, and likely work commitments but also providing childcare for their own grandchildren. Alongside juggling their own families and obligations, daughters are also expected to take on the role of caregiver for their mothers, placing a significant weight on their shoulders. This caregiving role encompasses various tasks, such as weekly shopping, chauffeuring to doctors, opticians, dentists, hospitals, accompanying them on shopping trips and cleaning to name a few. The daughter handles these responsibilities amidst her own busy life. However, when the prodigal son makes a rare appearance, a noticeable transformation occurs in the mother. She springs into action, fussing over him with great enthusiasm. Meanwhile, the daughter watches with a mixture of amusement and weariness, recalling the once-helpless mother who struggled to perform even basic tasks like boiling a kettle for a cup of tea. The sudden burst of energy and excuses about the son's busyness and importance leaves the daughter astounded as her once-incapacitated mother magically bends over backward for him. This stark contrast in treatment between sons and daughters highlights the unequal expectations and burdens placed on women within the family dynamic. It underscores the need for recognition and appreciation of the daughter's efforts and the importance of challenging these gendered roles.

Does this pattern sound familiar? Unfortunately, I have witnessed firsthand how this cycle of behaviour perpetuates itself. The grown-up daughter, influenced unconsciously by these dynamics, may unknowingly prioritise her own sons over her daughters, thus continuing the cycle of favouring males.

This favouritism toward males and undermining of females can also extend to women's mothers-in-law. One client shared with me the cruelty she experienced from her mother-in-law, who never showed her any kindness. It was a truly unpleasant family situation, with constant belittling. The aunties would gang up on her, particularly when she was a young woman and newly married into the family, simply because she would never be deemed good enough for her son. However, as the years went by and the mother-in-law developed dementia and required daily care, guess who stepped up to fulfil that role? The burden was placed on the wife of her precious son, not her own daughters. One might wonder, why would she care for a woman who treated her so poorly, looking down on her and causing numerous arguments and straining relationships over the years? The wife explained that she felt she had to "do the right thing." Perhaps it was a mix of guilt, a distorted sense of duty. A heartbreaking situation. The question remains, where does that guilt stem from?

These complex family dynamics and the internalised beliefs we inherit and perpetuate can have a profound impact on our choices and actions, even when it seems counterintuitive. It highlights the need for introspection, breaking free from societal expectations, and forging healthier and more equitable relationships within families. It is true that discussions about favouritism within families and the impact on sibling dynamics are more commonly focused on women's experiences. However, it's important to acknowledge that these dynamics can also occur in various contexts and affect men as well. While this book primarily explores women's roles and experiences, it's valuable to recognise the broader spectrum of family dynamics. In my own experience, having only a sister, I didn't have to directly compete with a brother for my mother's affections. However, my mother's sharp-tongued behaviour was directed towards both of her daughters. Yet, I always felt that her treatment towards me was in a league of its own. This could be attributed to my tendency to call her out on her behaviour and my refusal to unquestioningly comply with her demands. I have never been one to blindly accept things I don't agree with, and these characteristics are traits I strive to reinforce with my own stepchildren. I actively encourage them to question everything and not simply follow directives for the sake of it.

One of the most frustrating things my mother would use against me when she didn't get her way was claiming that I was never grateful enough. I never quite understood what she meant by that. As my mother, it was her choice to bring me into the world, which was her own desire. By making that choice, she also undertook the responsibility, along with my father, of providing a home, clothing, food, and all the necessities. So, the concept of gratitude felt misplaced in that context. These reflections on personal experiences with family dynamics serve as a reminder of the complex dynamics that shape our relationships and the importance of fostering critical thinking and assertiveness in the face of unjust expectations. Taking responsibility for our actions and recognizing how they impact others is indeed essential for our own happiness and well-being.

For instance, let's consider the context of going on a family holiday. Personally, I often found myself reluctant to participate in these trips due to the negative atmosphere created by my moody and difficult mother. Despite being told that I should feel privileged for the opportunity to travel abroad twice a year, I couldn't overlook the underlying tension and anger that overshadowed these experiences. In my mother's eyes, it seemed expected that I shared her values and thoughts on the matter. Disagreeing or expressing a different perspective would trigger her anger and nasty remarks.

Over time, I have developed a strong skill set in dealing with controlling individuals. I have learned that people-pleasing never leads to positive outcomes, and prioritising others' needs above our own can be detrimental to our well-being.

It's crucial to remember the wise words of *Lao Tzu: "Care about what other people think and you will always be their prisoner."*

By releasing ourselves from the burden of seeking constant approval and conforming to others' expectations, we free ourselves to live authentically and make choices that align with our own values and happiness. Taking responsibility for our actions includes embracing our own convictions and asserting our independence, even in the face of criticism or disapproval from others.

When examining family dynamics with a dominant matriarch or challenging mother-daughter relationships, we often observe the emergence of people-pleasing behaviours and this tendency is commonly associated with a lack of confidence. It is notable that it is predominantly women who fall into the category of people pleasers. While it is possible that some individuals have a predisposition towards being exceptionally cooperative due to societal norms, it becomes a concern when it consistently overrides their own well-being and becomes their default setting.

Many women who exhibit people-pleasing traits may not even know they are doing so. This can be attributed to the subtle indoctrination they have experienced throughout their lives. In the context of the common narcissistic mother dynamic, this may explain why people-pleasing tendencies are less prevalent among men. As a general observation, men often display more inner confidence and self-worth. The origins of this disparity could be attributed to upbringing and societal factors, or a combination of both.

Personally, I strongly believe in the notion of "the Queen eats first." And when I say Queen, I mean you and me. By this, I mean prioritising our own well-being and self-care. It is essential to recognise that we cannot effectively help or serve others if we are emotionally and physically depleted.

Don't just take my word for it, the signs are everywhere. The next time you are on an aeroplane, just listen to the inflight safety recording. 'Please ensure your oxygen mask is secured before helping anyone else'. It says beautifully that if you have nothing left in your tank, how can you be the best you can be to help? How can you serve others if you're knackered, resentful, burnout out and feel undervalued? Yet that is the life of many, amazing women. If we constantly feel exhausted, resentful, burnt out, and undervalued, it becomes challenging to lead fulfilling lives and positively impact those around us. Many incredible women find themselves caught in this cycle of self-neglect, putting the needs of others before their own. Recognising the importance of self-care and setting healthy boundaries is crucial for breaking free from the people-pleasing pattern and reclaiming our own well-being.

The connection between people-pleasing and anxiety is indeed significant. People-pleasers often believe that if they don't meet others' expectations or constantly seek their approval, they will face rejection or disapproval. This fear of not being liked or accepted drives their behaviour. Confidence does play a role in this dynamic, as people-pleasers often lack the self-assurance to assert their own needs and boundaries. Saying "no" becomes challenging because they fear it will lead to conflict or jeopardise their relationships.

The origins of people-pleasing tendencies can be multifaceted and vary from person to person. It is true that the desire to be liked is a natural instinct, rooted in our evolutionary history of living in tribes or groups and relying on the wider community for survival, however the development of people-pleasing behaviour extends beyond this instinct. It can be influenced by various factors, such as upbringing, cultural expectations, past experiences, and individual personality traits.

For example, individuals who were raised in environments where their needs and desires were consistently invalidated or where they experienced conditional love may internalise the belief that they must constantly please others to receive love and acceptance. Cultural or societal expectations that prioritise harmony and deference to authority figures can also contribute to the development of people-pleasing behaviours.

True altruism, which we know humans can demonstrate, does exist. However, it can only be classified as altruistic if you genuinely expect nothing in return. But then there is an argument that if you derive pleasure from giving, is it still altruism? I'll leave that for you to ponder.

Regarding kindness, acts of kindness fall within a wide spectrum. What truly defines "being kind," a phrase so commonly used, has been tattooed on my arm for many years as a constant reminder to myself, not to others. It's all too easy to get carried away with our own wants and desires. If you were to help someone without expecting anything in return and are at peace with that notion, that is true kindness.

I've had many instances where I thought someone was performing a kind act for me, but in truth, they expected something in return. If someone is pretending to be kind but has ulterior motives, I would rather know about it upfront and agree to it beforehand. That way, I can willingly decide if it's a fair trade or a giving situation in which I can receive with gratitude and grace. If this is not clear, then we are entering manipulation territory.

I learned a long time ago that not everyone would like me, just as I understood early on that no matter what I did, it would never be good enough for my mother. No matter how high I climbed the career ladder, how much money I earned, whether I owned my own detached house (something she often spoke about), or lived in a nice area (all of which I achieved by my early 30s), it would never be right. There would always be something else to criticise or pick at. So, I decided to follow my own path to happiness and see where it would lead me.

We understand that it's the journey, not the destination, that matters. When we fully own our lives, decisions, new experiences, mistakes, errors in judgement, and, of course, the great experiences, relationships, and fun times, we take full responsibility. This is the key to happiness. It eliminates excessive regret when we look back.

What is regret? It is the action or inaction that haunts us. Interestingly, research suggests that it is the inaction that lingers and causes the most sorrow. We ponder what could have been if we had stood up to our partners or family — would our lives have been better? The most constructive form of regret is when we reflect on our actions, learn from our mistakes, and use those insights to guide us forward. It builds confidence in our decision-making abilities, knowing that there is often a way around most situations. There is little to be done about the actions we didn't take or the opportunities we didn't seize.

We must never back down when demanding fair treatment, regardless of who is involved. We need to be aware of our blind spots and examine whether our actions stem from people-pleasing or genuine desire. Let's not be misled by the notion of the "sandwich generation" – everyone bears a fair share of responsibilities. If the burden falls solely on your shoulders, prioritise self-care before assisting others.

From a young age, we are indoctrinated with societal norms, but only by recognising and comprehending them can we break free from moulds for future generations of women.

Speaking of regret, one area where people are often told they will regret inaction is the decision not to have children. There is a prevailing notion that not having children will inevitably lead to profound remorse. But is it fair to use such a powerful emotion to sway someone's decision about childbearing? Join me in the next chapter as we delve deeper into this contemporary dilemma: To be a mother or not to be, that is the question! Together, we will explore the complexities surrounding this deeply personal choice.

Decoded 3
Children

Chapter 3

YOU'VE GOT TO BE KIDDING!

My mother worked as a midwife, so at a very young age—around 10 or 11—I distinctly recall her sitting me down to watch a video of a woman giving birth. It was a distressing experience, and if her intention was to dissuade me from considering pregnancy at a young age, it actually had a lasting effect! I've always been somewhat squeamish, so it was quite horrific for me. However, I'm happy to report that it didn't deter me from engaging in sexual activities ;-) Nevertheless, throughout my fertile years, I diligently took precautions to avoid pregnancy.

I started taking the pill at 14 and continued until my mid-20s when I switched to the depo provera progesterone injection, which I stayed on until my mid-40s. Only reluctantly did I discontinue it when I entered early menopause, and even then, I insisted that my husband undergo a vasectomy. I vividly remember my mother telling me that my Dad was my Nana's "menopause baby." At that time, in her mid-forties, she thought she was going through "the change" but discovered she was pregnant with her fourth and "miracle" child—my father! And I was determined to ensure that would never happen to me.

I can honestly say that I never actively analysed my lack of desire for children; it was simply not a conscious decision. In fact, I often recall the scene from *Sex and the City* where Charlotte proudly announces her decision to try for a child, and Samantha, in a perplexed and amused manner, asks, "Why?" That's precisely what I've always thought.

Only in recent years, particularly through conversations with my clients at the clinic, have I delved deeper into this question. Why do people want children? Or conversely, why do some choose not to have them? I understand that raising such questions can be controversial among many women, but let's seize the opportunity to collectively question, explore, and challenge the prevailing norms.

How dare a woman question her "whole purpose of being" on this earth? We have the power to challenge the unquestioned and explore thought-provoking territory. It is time to push the boundaries and engage in conversations that may cause discomfort but ultimately lead to growth and understanding.

I have heard women who choose not to have children being labelled as selfish, while others feel obligated to have children simply because it is expected of them. Many never even question if it is what they truly want and consider the implications of such a decision. I believe it is only through this courageous inquiry that we can pave the way for personal growth and societal progress. We must not be afraid to embrace the opportunity to question and thoroughly examine these significant matters.

In her remarkable book, *'Women without Kids,'* *Ruby Warrington* explores a thought-provoking subject. She initially contemplated titling the book 'Selfish C***s' but decided against it for obvious reasons. Ruby delves deep into the subject of women without children, highlighting the revolutionary rise of an unsung sisterhood. If you are interested in delving into the reasons why women choose not to have children, her book is definitely worth a read. Additionally, she hosts a podcast series with the same name, and you can find all the relevant links in the back of the book.

After reading this book, it made me deeply contemplate why I have never desired to have children. Reflecting on my upbringing with a controlling mother with whom I often clashed, I believe it greatly influenced my decision. Her insistence on making me watch birthing videos and her parenting style solidified my conviction that I would not repeat the "mistakes" she perceived herself to have made. She depicted motherhood as an unpleasant, thankless job that was financially burdensome and left her body in ruins (she never regained her figure). While I was unsure how I could be blamed for her post-childbirth body and the two harsh C-section scars that, back then, were straight down the middle of the abdomen rather than the neat bikini line scars we see today. She claimed her career was halted by us, despite her reaching the pinnacle of her chosen profession. Moreover, she believed I could never be grateful enough for the life she provided, the sacrifices she made, and so on.

In truth, I did share her sentiment that having children, even as a child myself, seemed restrictive, dull, tedious and stifling. I yearned to stand on my own two feet, have fun, earn my own money, and maintain control over my own destiny. Making the decision not to have children aligned with this vision. Conversely, I am grateful to my mother for providing me with a realistic understanding of the potential challenges involved in parenthood and for never imposing the expectation of having children upon me.

However, it is important for me to acknowledge that my perspective is just one among many. I recognise that women hold diverse viewpoints, each with their own unique desires and circumstances.

Some women yearn for motherhood and prioritise having children, while others face challenges in conceiving or have different aspirations and choose not to have children. I can only speak from my own lived experiences as I explore different circumstances, and I want to assure you that I hold no judgement towards my fellow women.

As I delve deeper into understanding my own choices and beliefs, it becomes evident that there is a vast spectrum of experiences and desires that encompass women's thoughts on motherhood. Whether women have steadfast expectations of having children or never anticipate it as part of their journey, each woman's circumstances are significant and deserving of recognition and understanding.

This chapter serves as a platform to shed light on the various perspectives surrounding women and children and how this subject can impact our lives and shape our identities, rightly or wrongly. By sharing my insights and passion on this topic, I hope to offer a glimpse into the complexity and depth of emotions that women navigate when it comes to their reproductive options.

Personally, I have always felt a stronger connection to animals than to humans. Throughout the years, I developed deeper and more meaningful relationships with our family dogs and my horses compared to other family members. For me, I didn't want to burden another person with the responsibility of being born.

I often wondered why my mother wanted children, and I distinctly recall asking her this when I was younger, probably under the age of 10. She proudly told me that despite not liking other people's children (a sentiment she is not alone in), she simply woke up one day, informed my father of her desire for kids, had her contraceptive coil removed (a strangely graphic and clinically driven detail to share with a 10-year-old), and subsequently became pregnant with my sister. Then, 18 months later, she had me, and that was it.

Despite all of this, I am certain that I possess genuine nurturing instincts, some may even call them maternal instincts. When it comes to my husband, my animals, my stepchildren, and supporting my fellow women, I feel a natural urge to provide care and support.

This brings us to another highly controversial question: Is Maternal Instinct a Myth?

This topic is regularly debated from both sides. I want to make it clear that I am in no way against anyone having children. I support women regardless of their choices because I believe it is about choice, not obligation. For me, the decision to not have children never felt like a conscious choice. It was more of an instinctual absence of thought over the years. It simply wasn't something that crossed my mind. To put it in context, it would be like explaining why I haven't become an astronaut; it just wasn't something I felt compelled to do.

Recently, the subject came up again during conversations with clients who don't have children and don't regret their life choices in this regard. This prompted me to research the topic further and speak to more clients who have chosen to have children, as well as those who haven't, to gain their perspectives on why they made their respective choices.

According to the *Oxford Dictionary,* the definition of MATERNAL INSTINCT is *"having feelings that are typical of a caring mother towards a child."*

I don't believe that maternal instinct is a myth. However, what I find incredibly interesting is how that instinct manifests itself.

The definition of INSTINCT itself is "a natural quality that makes people and animals tend to behave in a particular way using the knowledge and abilities that they were born with, rather than thought or training."

It is clear that we all possess instincts and have feelings toward other people and animals. Interestingly, women who work in therapy, therapeutic, or nurturing roles often display an abundance of this instinct. When we examine the role of healers throughout history, we find that they were predominantly women. Additionally, if we look at the witch trials, a majority of the women who were tortured and killed as witches, were childless, and many of them were village healers. For a more in-depth exploration of the witch trials from a gender and patriarchal analysis perspective, I highly recommend the book *"Caliban and the Witch: Women, the Body, and Primitive Accumulation" by Silvia Federici.* It provides a comprehensive examination of witch-hunting in Europe during the early modern period. *Federici's* book offers a compelling analysis of the witch trials through the lens of gender, patriarchy, and capitalism, exploring how the persecution of women as witches was linked to the rise of capitalism and the establishment of patriarchal control over women's bodies and labour.

To me, this historical context also contributes to the perception that women without children are somehow unnatural or wrong, leading them to be labelled as witches. It is ironic that these women likely brought great comfort to their communities, serving as local healers, nurturers, and potentially free thinkers who existed outside the social norms of the time.

They were feared by the men seeking to subjugate them. The belief was that by dominating and controlling feminine power (which they were so afraid of), men could harness women to be at their command and fulfil their desires. Creating fear quickly diminishes analytical and rational thought, as evidenced throughout history and more recently during the COVID debacle, where some people were more willing to comply with authoritarian mandates.

However, maternal instinct is different from motherhood. This is a separate conversation that warrants closer examination. If motherhood is being presented as an obligation for women, we must ask ourselves why promoting it would serve the interests of the patriarchy (I use this term to refer to an ideology, not necessarily men).

It is worth noting that many promoters or defenders of the maternal myth are indeed men. Therefore, we must question why and consider whether it benefits them at the expense of women. Some men have gone so far as to suggest that women should feel motherhood as their default setting, their natural purpose for being, or that it should not even be up for discussion if they do not want children.

I love this quote from *Minna Salami,* a feminist author and social critic, in her blog post titled *"The Mother Instinct":* 'The Mother Instinct is not merely about maternity or being loving and nurturing. Those elements have been glorified by male-dominant culture to keep women unthreatening. By depriving women of agency outside of the maternal, women are more easily relegated to serving patriarchal lineages through procreation and caretaking. But the Mother Instinct also informs women's subjecthood, as erotic beings, as creatives, as divine symbols, as people who protect, resist, revolt, and rebel.'

If you really think about it, the traditional role of women being at home and having children is very convenient. They are raising the next generation of taxpayers while their labour in running the home and raising children is largely unpaid.

In the US, paid maternity leave is still not a standard practice, and men taking parental leave is often frowned upon. In the UK, we are slightly ahead in this regard, but there is still a lot of room for improvement. The decision to have children may be made as a couple, but men don't have to miss a beat. Not much needs to change for them, while for women, everything changes and will never be the same again. In previous generations, it was more common for the village to contribute to raising a child. Society provided more support for women, often from other women. In later years, gender roles became further defined, with women staying at home, raising children, relying on their husbands for financial support, and getting on with it, whether they wanted to or not. Life was undoubtedly hard, but there may have been some comfort in knowing that living like this was the "norm" and not having to juggle a meaningful career alongside raising a family mostly on their own. During those times, there was likely a stronger sense of community among women who shared similar experiences. Without access to contraception and limited control over their bodies, daily existence, and even their own property, women stuck together and provided mutual support in childcare and other areas whenever possible.

Going further back, when people lived in closer proximity to their extended families, often within the same village where everyone was loosely related, the culture revolved around mutual support among kin.

In childbirth, there was a customary period known as the "Lying In," during which women who had recently given birth would have a bed rest period lasting from 2 weeks to 2 months. Female relatives, friends, and, if affordable, nurses would attend to them. This allowed the mother time to recover and establish a bond with her child before resuming her daily responsibilities. Moreover, the practice of assisting one another in daily life was commonplace, as most individuals remained local to their place of upbringing and had a readily available support network.

However, these days many women live away from their immediate family and may not necessarily have a solid circle of friends who are also mothers. Meaningful friendships often develop when one has their first child and begins to socialise within those circles. As a result, support may not be readily available from the outset.

Looking at the experience of giving birth today, one is fortunate to receive more than a day and a night in the hospital, even following a caesarean section. Back in the 1970s, the standard postpartum period provided by the National Health Service (NHS) was 10 days. I do not imply that life back then was necessarily superior. It was not. Women had limited autonomy in making life decisions and pursuing their potential beyond domestic duties and child-rearing. The lack of options must have been stifling, suffocating, and, for some, utterly soul-destroying. However, when we compare it to the present, we face a distinct set of challenges.

The pressure women can feel when making choices about having children, pursuing a career, or balancing both can result in increased hardship. Women are particularly affected by the decline in family life and diminishing social cohesion, raising significant questions. The illusion of choice for women now brings us back to the question of who bears the majority of the additional responsibility. It overwhelmingly falls on women. This reality is incredibly demanding and often thankless.

The concept of the "second shift" experienced by many working mothers is a tangible reality. They work a full day only to find themselves managing the majority of household chores and their children's schedules on top of their professional commitments. In the UK, while approximately 35% of women are now the main earners in their households, indicating some progress, we still observe that 45% of female breadwinners shoulder the majority of household and childcare responsibilities, compared to only 12% of male breadwinners. Additionally, male breadwinners are twice as likely to avoid any household chores altogether. The statistics clearly highlight the disparities. The average female breadwinner spends an additional 7.5 hours per week, equivalent to a full working day, on household duties, in addition to their full-time job.

According to *Professor Anne McMunn*, who led a 2019 study at University College London, women still shoulder a greater share of housework than men in 93% of British households, even when both parties are working full-time. These statistics clearly indicate that women continue to bear a disproportionate burden. While it is important to recognise that some women choose to take on this responsibility, *Professor McMunn* points out that this extra work is unpaid and often falls on women by default. She suggests that men's higher average earnings give them more bargaining power when it comes to negotiating household tasks.

This study is reflective of the prevailing situation in the UK, and I agree with *Professor Anne McMunn's* assessment that it is not necessarily a deliberate attempt by men to limit women's opportunities, however, it highlights the inertia of the status quo and the need for change. Additionally, across generations, women often witness their maternal role models shouldering the majority of household work, which reinforces the idea that this is the expected norm. Yet, it is disheartening to see ongoing uncertainty and inequality in the division of tasks within heterosexual partnerships. When even basic household chores are considered "women's work," it is no wonder that the responsibility of being the primary caregiver for children also disproportionately falls on women. Women face mounting pressure as societal expectations burden them with additional responsibilities. It is high time we challenge these outdated beliefs and strive for a more equitable distribution of duties in our relationships.

It is important to note that my exposure to same-sex relationships between women has been limited compared to heterosexual relationships. Therefore, my knowledge and research for this section of the book is primarily focused on the dynamics of a heterosexual relationship.

When listening to mothers discussing the changes in their bodies, the impact on their relationships with their partners, the challenges of difficult children, the financial costs, the loss of personal identity, the lack of sleep, and the derailing of careers, one might wonder, "What did you expect when you decided to have children?"

The situation is not helped by social media projecting an idealised and effortless image of motherhood disguised as advice or inspiration. Celebrities with their seemingly perfect post-birth figures, who may have used surrogacy or have an army of nannies and financial resources, perpetuate this unrealistic image. Why not acknowledge the truth that motherhood is incredibly demanding and exhausting, even for those with considerable support? This portrayal does not assist women who already feel the overwhelming weight of responsibility, exhaustion, and a potential lack of connection with their newborn.

Furthermore, it is disheartening to see a new father receive praise on social media for performing basic parenting duties such as changing a diaper or taking on small childcare tasks. These moments may be carefully staged for public display rather than reflecting everyday life. Such occurrences should not be seen as extraordinary but rather as an expectation of shared responsibility.

When women express their hesitation about wanting children, they are often met with a chorus of voices telling them they will regret that decision. However, what we seldom hear is the possibility of regretting having children, which is a genuine sentiment for some women. I have had women confide in me that if they had the chance to do it all over again, they would choose not to have kids. Of course, they still love their children, and their children are their world, but it is entirely possible to love your kids while not enjoying the role of motherhood itself. This is a natural and normal perspective.

Over the years, I have encountered numerous new mothers who are genuinely shocked by how challenging it is. One mother confided in me that while she expected childbirth to be difficult, she was completely unprepared for how demanding motherhood would be. She felt frustrated and taken aback that things didn't simply fall into place naturally. Even a year after giving birth to her beautiful son, she was still struggling with her mental health and hadn't experienced the instant love and bond she anticipated. It took around 10 months before she truly felt love for her child, despite her best efforts.

While everyone's journey is different, I believe this is a fairly common experience. Does this mean she lacked maternal instinct? Absolutely not. She was simply struggling to adjust to her new role as a mother. She desired to have a child (could that be considered maternal instinct?), but found the reality much more challenging than anticipated.

This is where the concept of "Feel Rules" comes into play. If a rule needs to be created for something, it suggests that it does not come naturally. The silent expectation that women will want to have a family, easily adapt to motherhood, or possess a natural instinct for it puts pressure on women and instils an unquestioning belief that they are meant to have children. Therefore, the issue of maternal instinct and the pressure to have children is not as straightforward as solely attributing it to the influence of the patriarchy. It is more about acknowledging that motherhood is an option for those who genuinely desire it.

But why do some women want to have children? Conditioning plays a significant role. Positive experiences with children, happy memories associated with them, and nurturing relationships with their own mothers can influence a woman's desire to become a mother. On the other hand, some women long for a family life they didn't have during their own upbringing, leading them to attempt to create their own loving family environment.

I once had a client who shared her story of losing her mother to alcoholism at the age of 15. Her father had long disappeared, and she found herself fending for herself. She became pregnant at 17 and had her daughter, which brought her happiness. However, her partner was violent and controlling. She fell pregnant again, this time with a boy, just a few months after giving birth to her daughter. Unaware of how easily a woman can conceive again so soon after childbirth, due to a lack of female guidance and support, she was coerced by her partner into keeping the baby. Now, she frequently advises her own children to seriously consider not having kids. While she wanted a child to have something of her own that nobody could take away, she confided that if she had the chance to do it again, she would not have had children. Once again, she loves her children, but not the role of motherhood.

Personally, I believe that I have much more to contribute to the world than simply reproducing and passing on my genes. I have always felt that I am enough, and the thought of being anything other than myself has never crossed my mind. In fact, I see my decision not to pursue the path of motherhood as a way of honouring those women who suffered in previous generations. Given that their only option was to get married and have children, I feel that I am honouring their memory by exercising my choice not to follow that path. We can't even begin to comprehend the suffering and suffocation they experienced when their options were so limited and they didn't truly have a choice.

I want to clarify that I always understood and respected the fact that motherhood was incredibly hard work and demanded a lot from women, not just during pregnancy but throughout their lives. It simply wasn't the path for me. Even during my years working in the corporate world, spanning from my mid-20s to early 40s, the topic of children would often come up during casual conversations and team events where we were getting to know our new colleagues. The dialogue would typically go something like this:

New Person: "Are you married?"
Me: "No, but I was when I was younger."
New Person: "Any kids?"
Me: "No, I'm far too young for kids."

Then, one day a new team member initiated the usual small talk. As I gave my usual response about being too young to have kids, I caught myself mid-sentence. As I was approaching my late 30s and changed my answer to "I'm probably too old" to have kids. It was a matter-of-fact realisation as I neared 40, and I found myself preoccupied with other matters, like attempting to run a half marathon before my 40th birthday (which I actually achieved at 39). Trust me, the three months of training for that was enough commitment for me.

I distinctly remember a woman at that work event, a few years older than me, who seemed to be lamenting the fact that her beloved son had moved out to go to university. She appeared to border on obsession, or dare I say, an Oedipus complex. She referred to it as "empty nest syndrome," and I couldn't understand why she wasn't looking forward to refocusing on herself and her husband. She had a love for travel, a nice home, and financial stability. Why wasn't that fulfilling enough? Growing up in a household where my mother never made any effort to hide her eagerness for us to move out (which I understood and appreciated since I valued my independence), I couldn't fathom why this woman felt so bereft at the prospect of her children leaving home after she had done her part in raising them.

Even during my brief marriage in my 20s, which, in retrospect, was probably not one of my best decisions, there were arguments about my husband wanting children and my lack of desire for them. Perhaps we should have had that conversation before tying the knot, but the thought simply didn't occur to me that I needed to explicitly state my disinterest in having children. I must admit that the idea of pregnancy itself made me feel oddly queasy, evoking images of that scene in *Alien* where *John Hurt's* stomach splits open and the baby alien bursts out. It repulsed and frightened me, solidifying my certainty that pregnancy was not for me.

But let's shift the focus back to society. I have witnessed countless incredible women tolerating infidelity and being with unsuitable partners, yet the ticking of their biological clocks grew increasingly loud, driving them to start families no matter what. Does this urge stem from frantic hormonal signals, compelling women to move forward? Or is it fuelled by a fear of missing out or regret? Could there be an inner voice reminding them that they will surely regret not having children? Are they succumbing to pressure from extended family or their own mothers or mothers-in-law? I hear all of these factors mentioned, but what I rarely hear is the influence of men in their lives, whether it's their partners or male friends. I have started posing this question to my close girlfriends: Why did you want children? And much like my clients, their answers are always different, often expressing that they didn't know; they simply felt it was the next step for them.

There are those who argue that if you don't have children, who will take care of you in old age?

However, we only need to look at the elderly people in care homes or those languishing alone in their own homes to see that having children is not a guarantee of care and support. Furthermore, when your children move away to pursue their own dreams and aspirations, can you expect them to drop everything and return to care for you? We should be raising independent adults who go out into the world to make their own mark. Surely the rule should be that your children are not responsible for you, especially if they have left home or started their own families, as their own well-being and that of their families should take precedence.

Needless to say, I am eternally grateful for all the women who have chosen to have children. I appreciate those who have embraced motherhood with ease, loving every moment, as well as those who have faced immense struggles, far beyond their expectations. I am also grateful to those who have been in privileged positions, whether financially or emotionally. Each and every one of you has contributed to the continuation of humankind, and I want to express my gratitude.

I hope that this chapter has prompted reflection, encouraging you to advocate for equality in your life's opportunities, to demand more support from those who have the means and responsibility to invest in your happiness. I also extend my gratitude to women like me who have chosen a different path, blazing trails and making unique contributions. We all have a part to play, and I thank you.

Above all, let us remember that we are all women, and we are on the same team. Let us strive to uplift and support one another, regardless of our choices and differences. In any given circumstance, let us ask ourselves if there is something we can do or say to propel women forward, to protect our rights and choices. Let us bridge our differences and foster a supportive and inspiring environment. Whether we choose to be mothers or not, we are all important and valuable members of society.

Decoded 4
Work

Chapter 4

WOMEN AND THE WORKPLACE

Women have made significant contributions to the workplace, and it's encouraging to see more women in professional and senior roles. However, despite the progress, there is still a lack of equal opportunities and concrete evidence of gender pay disparities. This raises the question: when women are told they can "have it all," is there an underlying subtext?

Perhaps women can have successful careers, but they fear they won't be able to have a family without being left behind or encountering difficulties with partners who may find the demands of their job intimidating. Or maybe women can juggle a fulfilling career, raise children, manage the household, and support their partners, but in doing so, they end up exhausted, disillusioned, and struggling in their relationships. This leads us to wonder if having it all is possible but not necessarily all at the same time. And if it is possible, why doesn't the same expectation apply to men who have careers and families?

If we contemplate the reasons behind this imbalance, a significant factor is the gender pay gap.

Why can't women be paid fairly and on par with their male counterparts? If they were, they would have more influence in negotiating a fair division of household and childcare responsibilities with their partners. Additionally, if both partners work, it would benefit women (who typically bear the brunt) if they could afford to hire domestic help such as cleaners, laundry services, or meal deliveries without feeling guilty.

Currently, we observe that women who work part-time or solely take care of the home often have to negotiate with their partners to secure financial support for such assistance. Even the structure of the working week does not have to conform to the rigid norms of antiquated workplaces lacking flexibility or compassion. In my own clinic, for example, I am open to employing women who can only work during school hours. It aligns well with our client base, as many of them are parents with children in school. Similarly, I prioritise avoiding rush hour traffic and allow flexible start times, including alternative weekend working. By embracing true flexible working, business owners can establish their own rules and create alternative structures that better suit their employees. The same applies to administrative staff who are not in clinical roles; whenever possible, I encourage them to work from home, even before the pandemic made remote work more widely accepted. I see no reason for them to endure rush hour traffic unnecessarily. If more employers explored flexible ways to structure the workweek and workdays, I believe we would have a happier and more engaged female workforce. It is often women who, once they become mothers, are forced to adapt their work to accommodate greater flexibility. Unfortunately, this often means accepting lower-paid or more menial jobs to effectively juggle their responsibilities.

Throughout my career, both in my own businesses and corporate roles, I have never understood why flexible working is seen as a challenge. During my corporate days, meetings and periods of uninterrupted work were common. At that level, we would delegate tasks to well-informed team members, enabling decisions to be made without constant involvement. Because we worked flexibly, there was no resentment when additional work or decision-making was required outside of normal hours. The belief that women structuring their hours around school runs wouldn't work is unfounded. I have seen it successfully implemented, where meetings were simply not scheduled during those times, treating the staff responsible for school runs as if they were in a meeting and couldn't be disturbed. Ultimately, what difference does it make if it's a school run or an actual meeting?

I was fortunate during my time in corporate sales because my performance, rather than the amount of time I spent at my desk, determined my success. The IT industry was an early adopter of flexible working, leveraging technology to enable it. Interestingly, it was often only senior male employees who felt comfortable being honest about their commitments, such as school runs or bath time, while senior women were less forthcoming for fear of not being taken seriously. I witnessed the old adage that women needed to be five times as good as their male counterparts and at least ten times as organised to feel they could compete.

As women, how can we initiate the necessary change to improve professional circumstances? We must challenge established norms at every opportunity. In *Vishen Lakhiani's* inspiring book, *"The Code of the Extraordinary Mind,"* he refers to *"Brules"* (Bullshit Rules) created by others to suit themselves. Although he primarily addresses other aspects of life and his entrepreneurial journey, this concept applies to all areas of life. I found his book to be greatly motivating.

In all aspects of our lives as women, we need to challenge traditional approaches, particularly in today's workplace. Working hours, standard practices, and general flexibility—all of it fails to support women in thriving, especially those with families. I must admit that earlier in my career, I believed it was primarily up to women to juggle everything if they wanted children because it didn't align with the business world. However, as I've grown older, it's clear that many of the structures we live within have been created by men to suit their needs. There is no reason why businesses couldn't offer flexible hours or lobby the government for increased childcare funding. Larger companies could even provide on-site creches to assist their staff. If practices like these became the norm, as they are in other countries, women wouldn't feel so burdened, stressed, and guilty.

It's not as simple as stating that men should take on school runs or household responsibilities, as the existing pay disparities act as significant obstacles. When we consider the immense amount of energy, capability, and juggling required of women in the workplace and at home, the decision to have children or not should be a genuine choice with ample options for flexible working and support from the home and community.

In previous generations, women worked, often from home during the industrial revolution, managing both their children and tasks such as textile or food preparation, in addition to running the household. Life was physically more demanding back then, even though it was less fast-paced compared to today. In this era, we are told that we can have it all—career, motherhood, and success. However, we still primarily bear the responsibility for running the home and caring for the children. Essentially, more burdens have been placed on our shoulders, introducing challenges unfamiliar to the trailblazing women of our parents' generation.

Recently, I spoke with a local hairdresser who pays £667 per month for 8.5 hours of nursery care for her one-year-old son, with a 20% government discount. Starting next year, once her child turns two, she will receive 15 hours per week of subsidised care. On the other hand, her friend who doesn't work will receive 30 hours per week of free childcare. Yes, you read that correctly.

Does this imply that the woman who doesn't work is considered a "good citizen," essentially unpaid labour to raise her children, while the working hairdresser is being punished? When the hairdresser had to work on an alternative Saturday, she had to rely on whoever in her family or friendship group happened to have children, without any structured support. She felt the responsibility for organising childcare always fell on her, not her partner. Moreover, she struggled to return to work due to the idea of leaving her new baby and the challenges of managing childcare and additional work. At times, she contemplated not bothering to return to work. The only thing preventing her from giving up was the fear of becoming too accustomed to being a stay-at-home mum, which would make it even harder to return to work with each passing month. She longed for adult company, financial independence, and a sense of freedom. She feared stagnating in her career and becoming a "boring mum" who would run out of things to discuss with her partner, as their conversations mainly revolved around their child since the birth.

We don't have to conform to these absurd rules where women barely break even and often have to claim they don't have a partner to qualify for government assistance just to get by. On the other hand, mothers on benefits receive housing, council tax, and other living expenses covered or subsidised, seemingly enjoying much more support and the ability to stay at home with their children. I can see which path seems easier for mothers. However, the solution is not to stay at home; the solution is to challenge these misogynistic and outdated societal norms. We no longer live in a supportive society with extended families or close-knit communities, and many women have no choice but to quickly return to work.

Now more than ever is the time to examine why women are being told that they should go back to work, that they are wanted in the workforce, but the actions of the UK government and society do not seem to mirror this and actively challenge it. If women are genuinely encouraged to work once they have had children, then there must be other ways to make this easier for them. Instead, the government's offerings to working mums fall far short of what is needed to assist them. Their policies seem to be put together without proper thought to the needs of working mothers, so the policies actually benefit the working mother who is setting an example for a future generation of workers.

I remember one night, having a conversation with my manager after a team meeting over a drink. Interestingly, she was a woman, which was relatively unusual in the industry. The industry was entirely male-dominated, although this particular employer had more equality policies in place. However, the old boys' club mentality still ran through it like an invisible seam. I was her right-hand woman and confidant regarding the day-to-day running of the team. During our conversation, she confided that probably four of our male team members (out of 11, with only 2 women) were often on a Performance Improvement Plan or PIP, which was an indication that their performance was lacking. Being on a PIP usually meant they were being given a chance to improve or find another job without going through a messy dismissal process. Surprisingly, these men just hung on, trying to achieve the minimum level of objectives in the PIP. She discussed the general lack of performance and made the point that if they were women, they probably wouldn't have even made it as far as being interviewed for the job. And if they had been lucky enough to be seen, they would have likely been offered internal administrative roles. She wasn't saying that she would discriminate against any woman applying, but rather highlighting the fact that their resumes wouldn't have even reached her, despite having the necessary qualifications required for that role. However, just by the fact that these men were already in their positions, any obvious gaps in experience or proof of poor performance were overlooked simply because they were men. These men were average performers who had been with the company for years and were afraid to move elsewhere because they feared being exposed for not being able to do the job. I hadn't really thought about it in these terms before, as I was focused on my own career and didn't like to dwell on negatives, but it was true. I wasn't angry or annoyed at those men because I knew them, and they were nice enough individuals. They fit the stereotype of nuclear family men, married with children, with their wives being the homemakers. Interestingly, they had the confidence to hold their positions, even though that confidence wasn't built on any particular career achievements. They simply didn't have any noteworthy deals or accomplishments that would put them on the map. Yet, they almost had an inbuilt sense of worth and genuinely believed that they deserved those job roles, which, in turn, meant they received opportunities for high-level positions and the associated sales targets and packages that came with them.

If we look at pay parity, it is disheartening that women are still underpaid for doing exactly the same work as men in this day and age.

A client of mine recently shared her experience of working as a psychotherapist in the NHS. She works 30 hours a week, balancing her job with managing her household and children, yet she receives, on average, 30% less pay than her male colleagues on a pro-rata basis. In fact, she sees more patients within her working hours, meaning her workload is higher. When she questioned this with her management, she was told that she held the same grade as the man who previously occupied the role. However, the previous male colleague actually saw fewer patients than her, and her current male colleague was on a higher grade while seeing the same number of patients.

How do we solve this? She is a professional woman with the same qualifications as her male counterparts and slightly more experience due to her age. She highlights the pay disparity but is given weak and ridiculous excuses to justify this type of pay and workplace discrimination.

In many cases, when hiring, especially when there is competition for good staff in certain roles, hiring grades will be adjusted to align with the market. However, this can result in a wage gap among colleagues.

I experienced this firsthand at one of the international IT companies I used to work for. I joined the company on a certain grade, but after a few years in the role, I noticed less qualified men coming in on a higher grade that had become the new standard due to market demand. Many of them dealt with less challenging accounts and didn't achieve the same high targets as I did. When I inquired about a grade increase to bring my salary in line with my male counterparts, I was told it couldn't be done because there were only so many available grades in the team. I was instructed to jump through a series of hoops just to be considered for a grade increase. At the time, I was still earning more overall due to my high targets and sales commission, so I convinced myself to see how it went.

After six months of "discussions" with my manager, I decided to leave because the injustice became too much for me, despite being a valuable team member who outperformed most of my colleagues and received multiple awards for my performance. I left and moved to a competitor, where I received a £15,000 increase in my basic wage and a higher overall package. After about 18 months, I was headhunted back to my previous company and returned with a £25,000 increase in my basic wage alone. This happened just 18 months after leaving because they wouldn't entertain a grade increase. I finally got my grade increase and a significant boost in my overall package, but I had to leave and come back to achieve it.

Despite being single and solely responsible for my mortgage, car, and personal expenses, I took matters into my own hands, as I had done several times throughout my corporate career. I was always confident in my abilities, and that confidence probably played a role in why I often earned as much as or more than my male counterparts. However, I was the exception. Some may argue that I acted more like a "man" in terms of advocating for myself, but throughout my years in the Information Technology industry, I had not seen men move as often as I did (on average, every 2 years) because they simply received pay raises when they asked for them while remaining in their current positions.

The underrepresentation of women in leadership positions and high-level careers can also influence women's choices. Without visible role models who have successfully advanced in their careers, women may struggle to envision a path that allows them to excel. Witnessing women achieve work-life balance without the level of sacrifice I have seen many women make when it comes to a successful career and motherhood would be incredibly encouraging. The lack of representation across the board can limit their belief in the possibility of achieving work-life balance and influence their career choices.

Motherhood is often associated with negative biases and penalties in the workplace. Women may encounter reduced opportunities for career advancement, lower salaries, and even discriminatory treatment based on assumptions that they will be less committed or less productive as employees after becoming mothers. These biases and penalties can discourage women from returning to work or undermine their confidence in their ability to effectively balance both roles. Furthermore, women who choose to prioritise their careers and return to work after having children may face societal judgement and criticism. They may be subjected to scrutiny, labelled as "neglectful" or "selfish" mothers, or accused of not prioritising their children's well-being. This social stigma adds additional pressure and guilt, impacting women's decision-making process and leading them to reconsider or postpone their return to work.

The time elapsed between returning to work often results in a crisis of confidence for many women, who fear that they have fallen too far behind in their chosen professions. They may even lose faith in their ability to re-enter the workplace at any level, especially if their home finances allow for it. This situation can become even more challenging if there is financial pressure, yet they find it difficult to face it.

There are various actions employers can take to address the gender pay gap and promote women in the workforce. It is evident that the issues holding women back are widespread, and perhaps a change in legislation is now necessary. One measure I would like to see is the requirement for employers to be transparent about wages and salaries, with this information displayed on job advertisements. Furthermore, I believe this should be taken a step further with legislative practices ensuring that individuals have the right to know what others in the same job are being paid. If there is a disparity in pay, it should be clearly outlined why that is the case. This would help all individuals in their careers by enabling them to understand how to improve their own prospects and contribute to the development of a more advanced workforce, which would benefit businesses as a whole. Additionally, removing standard questions about previous pay history could be beneficial, and legislation may help protect all potential employees in this regard.

Lastly, incorporating flexibility into job roles, where appropriate, would create opportunities for women to re-enter the workforce. It would be great if this also encouraged more men to equally share childcare duties, recognising the benefits of having flexibility in their own lives. However, we must acknowledge that childcare responsibilities often fall on women. Without the added pressures on women to return to work, providing this would make many feel more comfortable. By addressing flexible working or discussing limitations around working certain hours, they wouldn't need to feel like they are asking for special treatment, which is a common deterrent.

When we objectively reflect on our own careers, both past and present, it is hopeful to see some positive changes. However, there is still much work to be done in this area. Women bring exceptional qualities to the workplace, particularly in terms of empathy and emotional intelligence. Their empathetic, collaborative, and inclusive leadership styles, along with their resilience and holistic decision-making approach, contribute to their effectiveness in leadership roles.

Women leaders create inclusive, harmonious, and thriving environments that bring out the best in individuals and organisations. I can honestly say that some of the women I have had the privilege of working with as leaders have left an indelible mark on me. They have been true inspirations, teaching me invaluable lessons about both work and life. Now, it is our turn to pay it forward and support the next generation of women on their journey.

By lending a helping hand to pave the way for women to rise, I genuinely believe that our workplaces will shine brighter and become more inclusive for everyone involved. It is our duty to nurture and mentor, uplift and empower. Together, we can make a remarkable difference in creating a better, more vibrant future for all women in the workplace.

Decoded 5
Love

Chapter 5

HAPPY WIFE HAPPY LIFE

I've been with my husband for over a decade now, and I still have to pinch myself every day. I consider myself incredibly lucky to have found the man of my dreams. He's not only handsome, kind, sexy, and thoughtful, but he's also the funniest person I know. However, it wasn't always like this. I didn't meet him until I was 39, and let me tell you, I kissed A LOT of frogs before finding him. I had been married before when I was much younger.

As I grow older, I find myself reflecting more on intimate relationships, particularly the diverse set of expectations we have for a life partner. While I can only speak from the perspective of a straight woman, I am genuinely curious about this subject, especially considering the increasing reliance on dating apps for finding potential partners.

When I was in my late twenties, one of my friends was an early user of online dating. This was well before the clean, sanitised version we see nowadays on *Tinder, Bumble,* and similar platforms. These apps have turned the whole experience into a game, with mindless swiping left and right, mimicking the mindless scrolling of social media timelines. It makes dating feel disposable and impersonal. It's all about superficial judgments based on looks alone, without even considering shared interests or passions.

Back in the early noughties, it was a bit more involved. You needed access to your own computer or laptop and had to put effort into searching for a potential match. The quality of potential partners was probably similar to what we see on current dating apps, but the pool of talent was much smaller. Selfies were still a relatively new phenomenon, resulting in more realistic pictures. And if you liked someone, you had to strike up a conversation (no standard dick pics back then!). Anyway, going back to my late twenties, I had just ended a rather intense relationship. We lived too far apart, so we reluctantly split. To cheer myself up and get back into the dating scene, I decided to join my friend in exploring the relatively new world of online dating.

I was contacted by a seemingly sweet man who sent me a nice, funny, and courteous message. I was immediately attracted to his picture, which portrayed him with long, messy, sandy hair (I've always had a thing for guys with long hair). He appeared to be in his mid to late twenties, standing confidently in his wetsuit and holding a surfboard. And yes, we were a match! We chatted back and forth for about two weeks, discovering shared interests like our love for dogs and wine. We even had a few phone conversations. He seemed like the perfect person to help me get back on that dating horse, so we decided to meet up for drinks. The night arrived, and I drove nearly an hour to meet him at a charming country gastro pub in Lancashire. It was situated in the middle of nowhere, and I struggled to find it down the back lanes. It was summer, and the large, lush trees obscured the small entrance off the main road. I called him to help me pinpoint the turning. We were chatting on the phone as he guided me, and I turned into the pub's car park, ready to finally meet my date. Imagine my absolute confusion and horror when I was greeted by a completely different person — a fat, middle-aged man who was completely bald. He was dressed in a loud, baggy shirt that made him look pregnant due to his huge beer gut. Why was this man waving at me? Where was my long-haired surfer boy? Visibly shocked, I quickly turned off the car, grabbed my bag, and tried to compose myself, trying to hide the overwhelming disappointment behind a forced smile. As I stepped out of the car to confront this audacious "catfisher," he brazenly asked, without a trace of irony, "Saw your face then, is it the hair?" The hair was the least of my worries! He was about 50 years old (I was 27 at the time, and I always preferred younger men). He was ancient to me, and sadly, the figure standing before me was the exact opposite of what I found attractive in a man. It was an incredibly awkward situation. I politely had a drink with him, but I made my excuses and left. Yes, he was polite and good company, but I felt deceived. As nice as he was, he had completely misrepresented himself, and no matter how nice someone is, if you're expecting one thing and get the complete opposite, you're going to be disappointed, to say the least. I often wonder why anyone bothers with this strategy. "Catfishing" is now a common phrase, and that was certainly an early example of it. Why do people feel the need to hide who they are or, at the very least, not be truthful about their interests?

I like to use the example of business. In business, you must represent your brand honestly and consistently through everything you do. If you don't do that, you risk attracting the wrong clients. Imagine how disappointed you would be if you put up pictures of your work and your setup, but when clients arrived, they discovered a completely different place and the examples of your work weren't actually yours. It wouldn't take those clients long to realise the marketing was misleading, and if they stayed for their appointment, they would likely never return. So, if you play at being something you're not, you're out of alignment with your true brand. It's uncomfortable for both you and them, and it leads to constantly seeking new clients, which is not a great strategy for any business.

The same principle applies to our relationships. It might feel great to put our best foot forward, make an effort with our appearance, avoid saying anything too controversial on a first date, and find common ground as we would in any polite company. However, ultimately, if you pretend to be someone you're not, you won't be able to keep it up, resulting in the relationship not lasting... or so one would think.

Around that time in my life, I was earning well over £100,000 a year, and it created some unusual dynamics. Whenever I met a guy and they saw my house or car, they could see that I earned good money. And then, things would start to fall apart. It was either plain jealousy, a strange competitive vibe, or simply being on different wavelengths. I've always been hedonistic, strong-minded, and independent, and I cherished my freedom. One of the advantages of earning my own money and not wanting children was that I didn't have anyone to answer to, and I didn't have the overwhelming pressure of a biological clock ticking away. That being said, I've always believed that I would rather be alone than with someone who wasn't the right fit for me. So, I continued navigating through my thirties, struggling to maintain any meaningful relationship with a man. Of course, I acknowledge that I had my own work to do on myself, but for whatever reason, things just weren't falling into place.

I will never forget one day bemoaning my lack of a regular boyfriend. As much as I was having a lot of fun in my life with great friends, rewarding work, and enjoyable holidays, sometimes I longed for some nice male company. I wanted someone who truly understood me, someone I could go on a nice break with or simply go out for food and relax. But then came the advice from a well-meaning friend: "You need to tone it down a bit, Pen." I honestly didn't know what she meant, but she went on to explain how men don't like independent women. According to her, I should suppress my opinions, downplay my money and car (though I couldn't hide my house and car), and essentially become a submissive and demure woman. I was left speechless, realising how some women still held such beliefs.

In fact, when I assessed my friendship group at that time, I noticed that most of them were in unsuitable relationships. They seemed determined to get their boyfriends down the aisle, settling for guys who clearly didn't love or respect them. Many of these women had already experienced infidelity, but they put it aside to pursue marriage and, ultimately, start a family. I felt a sense of relief that I was not under the biological clock pressure when yet another ill-advised marriage happened within my friendship group. Controversially, I even asked my friends to stop inviting me to weddings because I didn't believe in lifelong commitment, especially in your 20s and 30s. I understood the expenses involved in weddings, and I thought they should give my place to someone who genuinely wanted to be there. Furthermore, I found weddings to be boring, tiresome, and formulaic. I wondered if anyone who married at that age honestly expected to remain with their first husband. Even if the man wasn't great, couldn't she have her children and then leave him? Personally, I had already gone through a divorce before turning 30, and I valued my financial independence. The idea of staying with someone for the sake of it seemed unthinkable to me.

Creating stability in my work and finances was crucial for me to have choices in life, including in relationships. I suspected that many of my friends believed that a potential partner's financial status was a major factor in their attractiveness as a potential baby daddy or husband, if they were lucky.

Interestingly, I developed a 5-year contract theory regarding marriage. I believe that couples could fall into the trap of taking each other for granted over time. The prospect of losing what you have can make you appreciate it more. So, what if marriage meant that after 5 years, the contract automatically expired? Only if both parties agreed to renew the contract would the marriage continue. If one or both parties didn't renew, the marriage would dissolve, and the assets would separate (though the specifics would require more thought, as I'm not a lawyer). Perhaps assets would never automatically merge, and only jointly acquired assets would be split. This arrangement would ensure that both partners were mindful of their commitment and would continuously discuss their relationship, roles, and responsibilities within the union. It may sound "anti-romantic" to some, but I strongly believe it would promote regular communication and prevent complacency and resentment. Everyday acts of kindness and a genuine investment in building a life together would become priorities.

In recent years, I've observed a strange submissiveness among younger generations, especially those in their 20s, when it comes to men. I always suspected I was ahead of my time. I pursued my career and did my own thing when it came to men. One of the privileges this brought me was the ability to be with the partner I wanted, without the pressure of his financial standing or career choice carrying me through. I was fiercely independent, and although feminism seemed to have lost popularity in my adult years, as it wasn't discussed much, I assumed it was because those values had become ingrained in female consciousness. Growing up with a female Prime Minister, our monarch, *Queen Elizabeth II* , and various other strong female figures, *Madonna* being a new, shocking yet fantastic role model for sexual liberation and forging your own path, it didn't occur to me that women couldn't demand more from life and their chosen partners.

It feels like we have regressed to a time where women are expected to be pretty, silent, and enduring. Is it because of the rise of social media and the ubiquitous nature of pornography? Perhaps it's a combination of both.

Pornography, in particular, often portrays a narrow and exaggerated representation of female sexuality, contributing to unrealistic expectations of body type, performance, and sexual behaviour. The constant exposure to carefully selected and enhanced performers can leave women feeling inadequate and constantly comparing themselves. Some even resort to seeking surgeries like breast implants or genital surgeries in the pursuit of conformity. It's disturbing that such surgeries are becoming normalised, and it's essential to teach our daughters (and sons) that genital diversity is natural and no particular appearance is superior or more desirable.

Equally troubling is the pressure on women to engage in sexual acts or behaviors that they may not be comfortable with or genuinely desire. Pornography often prioritises male pleasure, perpetuating an expectation that women should conform to it. This erodes their autonomy, diminishes their ability to express their desires and boundaries freely, and disregards their own sexual pleasure.

Like many others, my perspective on pornography has changed significantly as I reflected on it for the writing of this book. I've come to understand that the industry has ventured into increasingly extreme territory, prompting me to reassess my stance. It has shifted from consensual exploration to harmful power dynamics, exploitation, and degradation. Some pornography now perpetuates narratives that promote violence, objectification, and inequality. I cannot endorse an industry that normalises abusive behaviours and harmful gender dynamics, not to mention the damage it inflicts on the women involved.

We often hear that "sex work" is a woman's choice and empowering, but I have my doubts. I strongly recommend further reading on the prostitution debate, as well as other important issues for all women today, particularly *Julie Bindel's "Feminism for Women."* It is a must-read for all women.

Social media platforms also expose women to negative influences. The emphasis on physical appearance and the proliferation of carefully curated images contribute to feelings of inadequacy, self-comparison, and a distorted sense of self-worth. Women may feel pressured to present themselves in a certain way, striving for unattainable beauty standards perpetuated by filtered representations of perfection.

Furthermore, social media showcases seemingly perfect snapshots of couples' lives, highlighting romantic gestures, exotic vacations, and blissful moments with #blessed being a common hashtag. These images create an illusion of idealised relationships, leading others to compare their own experiences and feel like they are missing out. The truth is that the joy of long-term relationships takes on many different forms.

Finding joy in the simplicity of daily routines together, embracing imperfect moments, and navigating life's challenges as a team are the ingredients that bring profound depth to our relationships. The familiarity and intimacy that develop when sharing a bond of mutual love and respect are precious and grow stronger over time. Building a strong connection with your partner requires genuine effort and cannot be rushed. However, the stark contrast between the reality of everyday relationships and the carefully curated highlights shared on social media can breed unrealistic expectations for both women and men.

Online dating apps, while convenient, come with their own set of challenges. The swiping culture can contribute to a sense of detachment and emotional distance. It becomes a repetitive and impersonal process, reducing potential mates to a mere yes or no decision based on a few carefully chosen photos and a brief bio. This dehumanisation hinders the development of meaningful connections, preventing individuals from truly getting to know each other on a deeper level. Perhaps if finding dates required a little more effort, we would be motivated to work harder to establish genuine connections.

The constant availability of new matches fosters a "grass is greener" mindset, where individuals are always seeking the next best option instead of investing in building a connection with someone they have already matched with. This relentless pursuit of novelty poses challenges for relationships to evolve beyond the initial stages, as the allure of finding someone seemingly more appealing with a simple swipe can hinder the commitment and effort required for relationship growth.

When I hear my clients talk about their frustrations with online dating, I feel relieved that I am in a solid, happy marriage and don't have to rely on it myself to find a partner. However, I did give online dating another try just before I met Phil when I was in my late 30s. Throughout my 30s, I had an on-off boyfriend whom I kept going back to like a boomerang. This was mainly because my options for potential partners were limited at that age, as many people were pairing up, getting married, and having children. I knew deep down that he wasn't the right person for me, so I decided it was time to move on.

During that time, online dating seemed like the obvious choice, and back in 2013, the app everyone was using was *Plenty of Fish*. Surprisingly, I seemed to attract a steady stream of 22-year-olds, despite being

39 at the time. I must confess that I even went on a couple of dates with one of them, which was fun initially. However, it came to an abrupt halt when I went to pick him up one night and witnessed him having a heated argument with a woman who appeared to be my age. It turned out to be his mother, who approached me and informed me that he was grounded. It made me suspect that he had lied about his age, especially when I saw her give him a clip around the ear. It was a disappointing experience.

Around that time, I had taken up running as a new hobby, perhaps as a way to channel my sexual frustration into something other than just dating. I decided to train for the Wilmslow half marathon with my friend. Despite having large breasts, I found that I was picking up running quite well and enjoying my training. When I created my profile on the dating app, I even included a picture of myself participating in a park run. Despite being a size 16, I have always been body confident. I was fit and healthy, and I firmly believe that there is someone out there for everyone.

I included some nice headshot selfies along with a couple of pictures of me running. After the terrible catfishing incident a decade earlier, I was determined not to misrepresent myself. I had nothing to hide. Among the numerous messages from younger men, there was one guy in his early 30s who caught my attention. We exchanged messages for about a week, although I wasn't overly enthusiastic about him. However, he persisted in pursuing me, and considering the lack of other viable options at that time, I was contemplating meeting him for a date. But then, during our polite exchange, I had my first experience of gaslighting by a potential partner. He suddenly asked, "Can I just check, what clothes size are you?" It was such a strange question. I replied, "I'm a size 16." He responded, "Well, I've been doing this workout program called Insanity, and I'm in the best shape of my life, so I think I'm going to need someone thinner." I calmly replied, "That's fine. I'm actually training for a half marathon at the moment and I'm also in the best shape of my life. I totally understand, as I also prefer slim guys. Good luck in your search!" He then messaged me saying he would make an exception for me, but I decided to block him.

You see, I have never tolerated that kind of disrespectful behaviour, not then, not now, not ever. I have never believed that my worth is determined by my weight, and for most of my life, I have been fit and healthy. I value other aspects of myself, and I genuinely like who I am as a person. I have always had a lot of confidence. I also firmly believe that we should never need to misrepresent ourselves in any way, shape, or form. Those who appreciate our mind, body, disposition, and general vibe will find us as long as we stay true to ourselves. That's when we meet our true match in every sense of the word.

Remember, our feminine power resides within all of us, manifesting in various ways. When we tap into our power, our sexual divine, embracing our raw and beautiful selves, we connect with a depth of transformative qualities. I believe that once we awaken our abundant energy and recognise that our sexual pleasure can be awakened within us, it opens doors to unlimited opportunities in work, happiness, and life. We must confidently step into this realm and refuse to be objectified solely for the pleasure of others. Through the integration of our feminine divinity, we are free to embark on a journey of self-discovery and self-acceptance, healing past wounds, and embracing our inherent worthiness and beauty.

Once we understand that we all deserve a committed and loving partner, someone who can openly and honestly communicate about anything and everything, we can build a partnership based on mutual respect, equality, and shared values. A true partner supports and values our opinions, is open to new experiences, challenges us, and stands by our side.

Together, we can grow as a couple, creating a world where both individuals thrive. Accept nothing less than what you deserve.

Decoded 6
Menopause

Chapter 6

THE CHANGE IS GOOD

We all need to blow off steam and decompress from time to time. In America, many people have Psychotherapists who fulfil this role by providing a listening ear without judgement or advice. In my work with women, whether in my clinic or business coaching, I embraced this role of being a supportive listener. For many women, it can be challenging to complain about their lives, especially to their partners, children, or friends. Sometimes, the topics they want to discuss are deeply personal and cannot be shared with family or friends. Menopause often became a prominent subject, as well as venting frustrations about their husbands or talking about their hopes and dreams. I understand that some women might say they are tired of hearing about menopause, but for me, it is an important topic because it affects the lives of many women, including my own.

Menopause is a phase that we will all go through in one way or another, and thankfully it seems to be spoken about more these days. This increased dialogue is largely due to several influential women who have spoken up about their experiences. I remember the first person I heard speaking openly about menopause was *Meg Matthews*, closely followed by *Davina McCall,* who remains at the forefront of the conversation. Since then, many others have joined in sharing their stories. It's not just a social contagion but a reflection of our longer life expectancy. Simply put, we live longer now than in the past.

The reduction and cessation of vital hormones in women occurs because, hundreds or even thousands of years ago, our life expectancy was much shorter. Women would typically only live into their 30s, 40s, or 50s. Once they had replicated their genes and given birth to children, there was no further need for those hormones. The goal was to have as many children as possible, given the high child mortality rates at that time, in the hopes that a few would survive to continue the species. Women would rear their children until they reached their early teens, at which point they could start having offspring of their own. After that, their purpose was fulfilled, and they could pass away. So, the hormones were no longer necessary for procreation, as that was the primary reason for their existence. That's the simplified explanation.

For me, I entered perimenopause around my early forties, and I remember feeling quite awful during that time — my energy was drained, and I felt out of sorts. Many of my clients were around the same age as me, and they were either approaching menopause or were already going through it. It was a hot topic of discussion, pardon the pun.

Looking back, I do recall experiencing perimenopausal symptoms, though I wasn't aware at the time that it was the beginning of my menopause journey. I sensed that something wasn't quite right — I couldn't quite put my finger on it. I wondered if it was just my age, if my brain was finally slowing down. I struggled with multitasking, which used to come easily to me. But now, I know that it all started around the typical age for perimenopause, which can begin as early as the mid-thirties but usually occurs between the mid-forties and fifty. The average age of menopause in the UK, according to the latest studies, is 51.

My understanding of menopause deepened when I began working with an amazing new client named *Simone*, Nutritional Therapist who specialises in Menopause. At first, I found her specialisation to be an odd choice and wondered if there was much demand for it. However, as I continued to work with her, I learned so much, and it gradually dawned on me that I was, in fact, going through my own menopause journey at the age of 46.

I had been using Depo-Provera as my chosen form of contraception for over two decades, and it was perfect for me. Every 12 weeks, I would receive a quick jab in my backside, and I would be free from periods and mood swings. It was a solution that worked wonders for me. I believe it helped me maintain focus and even overachieve in my business life by providing stability and freeing me from the worries of hormonal fluctuations and periods, which many women experience.

During my younger years, I suffered from terrible premenstrual tension (PMT), mood swings, and heavy periods. I started using birth control pills in my teens, which provided some relief, but at the age of 25, I decided to try Depo-Provera, and I never looked back.

When I turned 35, I had a check-up with a female consultant at St. Mary's Hospital to assess my bone density and other markers, and fortunately, everything was fine. The consultant mentioned that she had never encountered someone who had been on Depo-Provera for such a long time since women typically come off it to start a family. I asked if I could continue using it until after my menopause, and she agreed. She also shared that other women had told her similar stories about how controlling their monthly mood swings had given them an edge in life and business, allowing them to stay focused and not be slowed down by monthly bleeding. I had no desire to have periods. I believed life was too short, and I never wanted children so it was a perfect solution for me.

At the age of 44, I experienced a real disturbance in my life. I had just returned from a family holiday in the UK, a lovely, relaxing week spent at a friend's holiday home with my step-kids. Everything seemed fine and there was no reason to worry, yet I had an overwhelming sense of impending doom. It was a strange feeling for someone who had never suffered from anxiety or depression. I initially thought I might be coming down with an illness. Upon returning to work I shared my feelings with another client who happened to be a therapist. I described the strange post-holiday feeling I had experienced, and she identified it as anxiety—an impending sense of doom. I was puzzled because I had noticed some ups and downs in my mood. I remembered snapping at my stepkids over a minor issue, and it felt awful as it was an overreaction and out of character for me. I was definitely feeling out of sorts.

Recognising the need for guidance from an expert, I reached out to Simone and she graciously agreed to become my menopause coach. She introduced me to a remarkable hormone testing method called *DUTCH,* known as the gold standard in the field. Simone shared her frustrations with the FSH test commonly offered by general practitioners, dismissing it as ineffective. Her own disappointing encounters with doctors had motivated her to take control of her health during her perimenopausal phase. She had faced the all-too-common dismissive response from doctors, who often suggested antidepressants instead of addressing the root causes. Determined to find a solution, Simone embarked on a personal journey of self-discovery, which led her to India. There, she immersed herself in the wisdom of Ayurvedic practices and progressive approaches to health and fitness. Through this transformative process, she not only shed the weight she had gained during perimenopause but also achieved her best-ever state of health, all without relying on hormone replacement therapy (HRT). Inspired by her own experience, she went on to help many other women navigate this confusing phase of their lives. Having Simone as my guide gave me reassurance and support during this significant period of transition.

Another common trend is the prescription of antidepressants for women experiencing symptoms that are likely related to menopause. It is important to question the suitability and reasoning behind prescribing antidepressants for hormonal imbalances. It's worth noting that some doctors may be influenced by substantial incentives from pharmaceutical companies to prescribe specific drugs. For further reading on the subject of incentives for doctors regarding commonly prescribed drugs like statins, I recommend *Dr. James La Funu's book, "Too Many Pills."*

Simone helped me arrange a DUTCH test, and I was eager to find out what was happening inside my body. Stopping the Depo shot was a significant decision for me. My perimenopause had led to a drastic decrease in my sex drive and caused hip pain, making me feel miserable yet I was afraid to have sex, fearing the possibility of getting pregnant at my age.

As I reflected on the years of using hormonal contraception, I wondered why it seemed like the only viable option for women. These medications are often prescribed without fully understanding their long-term effects on our bodies. For example, prolonged use of Depo Provera can lead to bone density problems, and women are often advised to discontinue the pill after a certain period for health reasons.

The constant cycling of hormones can make women feel trapped, prompting me to explore the pros and cons and consider alternative options when I decided to stop using hormonal contraception for the first time in about 30 years. On one hand, hormonal contraception empowers women by providing control over their reproductive choices. I empathise with the struggles faced by women who came before us, who had limited options and were judged harshly for their sexual choices and pregnancies. However, it was disheartening that once again, women had to rely on hormonal medications. These hormonal medications, such as the contraceptive pill, Depo shot, implant, and Mirena coil, are not particularly sophisticated. We may wonder if they affect us in ways we are unaware of, including their impact on our sex drive. Even if we were to consider trusting our male partners with hormonal contraception, could we ever fully rely on its effectiveness?

The easy answer to whether we would trust our partners with this responsibility is no. As mentioned earlier, the stakes are much lower for men when it comes to pregnancy, especially if it is unplanned. This was particularly relevant in my situation, as I was trying to determine whether I was in perimenopause, menopause, or post-menopause.

On the other hand, obtaining contraception was easily accessible to me from the age of 14. It was readily provided, and I was grateful for it as I didn't want to get pregnant. However, when it comes to getting hormone replacement therapy (HRT), especially the bio-identical variety for hormone deficiencies that significantly impact women's lives, the process can be much more challenging.

After undergoing the DUTCH test, I was astonished by the results. At 46 years old, my progesterone and oestrogen levels resembled those of a 60-year-old woman. It made me wonder how I was functioning. The test also revealed irregular cortisol levels, which spiked at inappropriate times. Working long hours in the clinic, relying on painkillers to get through the day, and neglecting self-care had taken a toll on my body. I couldn't lose weight, and I felt overwhelmed. The test also shed light on how my body metabolised oestrogen, indicating the different pathways it could take, some safer than others. Although my testosterone levels seemed relatively high, I suspected I'd always had naturally higher levels throughout my life due to my overall happiness, confidence, and voracious sexual appetite. However, without sufficient oestrogen, I wouldn't experience the full benefits of my natural testosterone levels. The test results were fascinating, and despite the £300 cost, it was money well spent. I discussed the urgency of starting HRT with Simone, who supported my decision. She provided me with the names of bio-identical hormones to ask for, advised dietary changes, and encouraged me to take time off and slow down.

Following her advice, I made positive changes, and my weight started to decrease. I began feeling more comfortable in my own skin, but getting HRT was still a priority. All of this occurred in late 2019 and early 2020, just before the pandemic hit. I was also waiting to receive a steroid injection for the chronic pain in my hip and back that had accompanied my hormonal changes. The constant, debilitating pain was a new experience for me, and there were days when I would sit and cry. My mood was frequently irritable, and poor Phil bore the brunt of it at times, coinciding with my efforts to obtain HRT.

I had a standoff at my GP surgery when I attempted to make an appointment to discuss HRT. I had been trying to call for a couple of days but didn't have the time to wait on hold for 40 plus minutes. So, I decided to go to the surgery in person the next time I was out and about. Luckily, the waiting room was fairly empty when I arrived.

"I'd like to book an appointment with a doctor, preferably on a Friday, to discuss my HRT," I politely requested.

"Was it an emergency?" the receptionist inquired.

"Well, no," I replied, "not in the biblical sense of the word. I'm not seriously ill, but I really need to schedule an appointment to discuss getting on HRT as soon as possible. I feel pretty awful most of the time."

The receptionist, with a dismissive look and her gaze fixed on the monitor, offered me a series of random dates throughout the week, none of which were Fridays as I had requested. This was before the pandemic when working people typically couldn't just drop everything and go to the doctor as many were not working from home. I explained to her again that I needed a Friday since it was my day off and I couldn't easily rearrange my work schedule. She responded with another eye roll and provided unhelpful dates that didn't align with my request. I paused to read her name badge and said,

"What exactly is the problem here, Melanie?"

"Well, you say you need to see someone, but you're being difficult," Melanie replied.

"Difficult? Do you assume that everyone is sitting at home all day, not working?" I retorted.

"Alright then, can you look at the diary and book me for a Friday in 2-4 weeks' time?"

Melanie snorted derisively. "We don't have the diaries that far in advance," she said, looking at me with pity as if I were making an unreasonable request.

"Why not?" I asked.

"Well, we don't know if the doctors will be on holiday," she explained.

"How utterly ridiculous," I exclaimed. "At my clinic, we allow booking up to 3 months in advance, taking into account holidays and cover. Instead of this tedious exchange, how about implementing an online booking system? It's 2020, and you still can't book a doctor or nurse appointment online?"

Melanie snorted again and rolled her eyes, condescendingly saying, "We are the NHS, you know. It all costs money."

"Don't give me that," I responded. "You know as well as I do that GP surgeries are not technically part of the NHS. While you may be paid by them, you're not them. And what kind of excuse is that for not having an online booking system? It's not free. My taxes pay for this service, and I have no option to opt out. The least you could do is make it easy for working people to see a doctor at their convenience. Why aren't you open on weekends? It's just so much easier to have an online booking system and be open when your customers need you because we are customers. This is a commercial enterprise, just like my business. It's not that hard. We've always had online booking, and our busy clients love it."

At this point, realising that the ruse was up, and I knew they weren't technically part of the NHS, Melanie suddenly found some available dates for me on a Friday and out-of-hours, quite conveniently.

"Well, there are other surgeries we use for out-of-hours, just not here. There's one in Fallowfield," she said.

"Fallowfield is fine, as long as it's on a Friday," I fired back.

Contrary to popular belief, these GP surgeries are not truly part of the NHS. While they may present themselves as such, they are actually businesses. They earn money from each and every one of us and often promote certain drugs they receive incentives for from pharmaceutical companies. It's important to question them and not take everything at face value.

Melanie's demeanour had softened somewhat, almost as if I were dealing with an actual business with a customer care process. She then sheepishly provided me with a list of available dates at various locations in the area, and I easily booked an appointment for the following week on a Friday afternoon with a doctor located just 10 minutes away from the surgery, in Fallowfield. Many people can likely relate to this exchange as it is unfortunately familiar.

Within our healthcare system, we find ourselves trapped in a patriarchal structure that limits our options and hinders our well-being. *Dr. Mindy Pelz* explores this intricate web of patriarchy in her book, *"Fast Like a Girl,"* providing a comprehensive analysis of the subject. In her enlightening work, she delves into the mechanisms through which patriarchal influences shape our experiences in the realm of health and wellness. For a more in-depth exploration of this pervasive issue, I recommend reading *"Fast Like a Girl"* and uncovering the insights it has to offer on the wider topic of fasting health benefits, specifically from a female perspective.

Dr. Mindy emphasises the cultural acceptance of women suffering, and I couldn't agree more. It's no surprise to hear that suicide rates peak among women between the ages of 45 and 55. I've personally experienced my lowest points in my late 40s when I struggled to balance my hormone levels due to changes in my HRT. I used to take for granted the energy and vitality of my younger self. I would leap out of bed, full of enthusiasm, without feeling any pain or aches. I was eager to start my day and had a voracious appetite for what lay ahead.

I recently met with a close friend who, like me, had worked as an Account Director in the IT industry before both of us decided to leave in our 40s. Although we only became acquainted after venturing into self-employment, we quickly discovered that we shared a similar outlook on life. We had both experienced the fast-paced and luxurious lifestyle of the corporate world, enjoying the perks of money, cars, and travel. But we were fully aware that leaving behind that cushy existence and embarking on our own entrepreneurial journeys would come with its own set of challenges and require hard work.

However, one challenge we hadn't anticipated was the significant drop in energy during perimenopause. In our corporate roles, we never had to question the level of energy needed to keep up with the demands of the job. But when perimenopause hit, and our energy levels declined, it caught us off guard. When we both transitioned to self-employment in our 40s, we approached building our respective businesses with the same enthusiasm, work ethic, and drive that we had exhibited in our corporate roles. Up until the pandemic struck, our businesses were thriving. However, the pandemic dealt a severe blow to our hard-earned achievements over the past decade. Suddenly, in our 50s, we found ourselves without savings or a substantial pension. Despite being strong and resilient women in positive romantic relationships, we both felt miserable during menopause.

This made us wonder how women in more challenging circumstances cope with menopause. Women who are more timid, lack support, or find themselves in difficult relationships may feel isolated and unable to discuss their experiences with friends. We had already experienced the daily struggles of trying to find a balance between rest and self-compassion while also dealing with concerns about weight gain and exercise on top of managing our businesses. It was an exhausting ordeal.

Fortunately, there is now more research available on menopause, and one area that particularly interests me is insulin resistance. As women experience oestrogen decline, they become more insulin resistant, which can lead to weight gain commonly referred to as "middle-aged spread." However, I dislike this term as it implies an inevitable outcome. Many of us tend to follow eating and exercise patterns that may have worked for us when we were younger, and when they no longer yield the same results, we blame ourselves and feel disappointed and like failures. Simply being told to move more and eat less is not helpful advice. The complexities of gradual weight gain are nuanced, and there is no one-size-fits-all approach. When our joints start to ache, engaging in high-energy cardio and intense workouts may not be the best option if we're not feeling up to it.

Fat-shaming rarely leads to positive outcomes. Understanding and empathy, on the other hand, go a long way. Like my friend and me, most busy women, particularly at our age, are constantly juggling multiple responsibilities and running around. It's easy to fall into the habit of eating on the go. As our blood sugar levels rise, our joint pain worsens, and our essential hormones, including testosterone, decline, it's no wonder that women feel like they no longer recognise themselves. When someone who has always been motivated suddenly struggles to go for a walk or plan healthy meals for the week, they may feel lazy or attribute it to simply "getting old." This loss of confidence can be accompanied by other lesser-known symptoms of menopause, such as anxiety, night sweats, hot flashes, and brain fog. Trust in one's own judgement diminishes, and it's understandable why many women choose to leave the workplace in their forties.

I urge every woman who feels out of sorts, experiences unexplained anxiety, or has any of the symptoms I've described to consult with their GP and consider starting hormone replacement therapy (HRT). Please don't wait until your confidence is shattered, your relationships suffer, or you struggle to hold down a job. Keeping hormone levels balanced through HRT is crucial. Personally, I believe that if I had started a year earlier, my own nerve pain in my back and hip, which has plagued me throughout menopause, might not have been as severe. I consider myself fortunate to have had someone to guide me through that challenging time. I have also found that reducing sugar and alcohol intake has been immensely helpful. Becoming a moderate drinker who can go months without a drink is an accomplishment I never thought I would achieve, but I am delighted that I made that change.

One of the game-changers for me, and perhaps the key factor that allowed me to find the energy and mental clarity to write this book, was starting testosterone therapy. I knew that there was still a missing piece of the puzzle for me. After a couple of years on bio-identical oestrogen and progesterone, despite hearing other women rave about how it transformed their lives, I didn't share the same sentiment. While my night sweats and irritability had improved, my energy levels and libido were not showing much improvement, even after delving into tantric sex during lockdown (which I wholeheartedly recommend!).

Getting prescribed testosterone wasn't initially straightforward, and the conversation with a young male GP about my sex drive was somewhat amusing, albeit a little awkward. He was clearly uncomfortable, doing his best to navigate the topic. Of course, I hold nothing back and have no shame, especially when it comes to matters of sex and, in particular, with my husband. I could sense his cringe and stammering on the phone as I vividly described the changes in my libido. Looking back, it's a good thing it was only a phone consultation! Currently, the guidelines regarding testosterone for menopausal women are woefully outdated, focusing primarily on sexual function. Now, call me cynical, but I can't help but think that these guidelines are more driven by a desire to help the men in our lives rather than us women. Nevertheless, to provide you with the latest information, here are the *UK NICE guidelines for testosterone in menopausal women:*

Altered sexual function 1.4.8 Consider testosterone supplementation for menopausal women with low sexual desire if hormone replacement therapy (HRT) alone is not effective.

I find this guideline mildly insulting. While it's true that libido can plummet in some women, myself included, there are other equally important factors to consider when it comes to testosterone. In my experience, it has helped reduce brain fog, increase energy levels, enhance mood, and even improve muscle tone. If you're interested in delving deeper into the subject of testosterone and its effects on both men and women, I highly recommend reading *"T" by Dr. Carole Hooven.* It's a fascinating book that provides enlightening insights. *Dr. Hooven* also features in several podcasts on the topic, in case that's your preferred way of consuming this type of content. It's worth noting that she is a Harvard evolutionary biologist, so keep that in mind—it's not exactly light holiday reading, but incredibly interesting nonetheless.

When it came to my own pursuit of testosterone, it was ultimately my female GP who took charge and quickly resolved the issue. This was after the male GP had suggested I be referred to a specialist clinic with waiting times of 4-6 months for a telephone consultation! I questioned the need for such a laborious process since I knew many of my clients had already pursued the private route and were often prescribed testosterone without extensive blood tests. I should mention that these women had paid, on average, £200 for a private consultation and were then faced with monthly private prescription charges of around £75, on top of the cost of testosterone. It was a double blow that in 2022 (at the time of my quest), testosterone couldn't be routinely prescribed on the NHS.

The reality wasn't as complicated as the male GP had made it out to be. I argued that I could simply start with a low dose, see if it improved my symptoms, and adjust the dose accordingly. He proceeded to lecture me on how it was much more intricate for women. I immediately pointed out that women already have testosterone, so it was hardly an unknown factor, it's basic biology. I also mentioned that I had heard that men could undergo a blood test at the same GP surgery and receive a prescription promptly.

As luck would have it, a few weeks after my conversation with the young male GP, a female GP from my practice called me out of the blue. She was truly amazing. We discussed the matter, and she promptly arranged for a blood test that week. Just a week later, I had my first prescription for testosterone, and I felt happier than I had in years. She provided me with the dosage and parameters based on the guidelines, but also encouraged me to find the dose that felt right for me. Let me tell you, this has been a game-changer for me in terms of feeling somewhat better. Particularly at the higher end of the dose, I noticed my libido returning after about a week, increased energy, a natural inclination to be more active, and an improvement in my muscle tone, nothing drastic, of course, but I felt firmer. I also experienced an overall sense of improved well-being and felt a glimpse of my old self returning.

Often in the clinic, I hear women proudly proclaim that they have managed without hormone replacement therapy (HRT), and I am astounded. Recently, I had a new client who sat before me with dry and sensitive skin, well above her usual weight, and tears streaming down her face. She shared how she had reached the age of 55 and managed without HRT, except for her persistent brain fog. Interestingly, during our conversation, she would frequently forget what she was talking about. She admitted she was forgetful and it was causing frustration and hindering her business as a professional consultant. Is that truly what we define as "managing"?

Unfortunately, this is an all too common occurrence. Many women enter perimenopause or early menopause, and those dreadful feelings start to creep in. I hear countless women expressing sentiments like, "I just feel off," or "I haven't been happy lately," or "I've been experiencing intense anxiety."

Why does the myth of powering through persist? Why should women believe that they should simply "manage" without seeking help? It's as if there's an obligation to endure silently, fearing that complaining or acknowledging their true feelings would let others down. Perhaps this self-doubt is the beginning of the lack of confidence that plagues so many middle-aged women. Do they receive applause for not needing hormonal assistance during menopause? Absolutely not.

Based on my own experiences and conversations with other women, I believe that "getting through it" without some form of help or intervention is unrealistic. After all, don't we experience changes in our physiology and associated hormone deficiencies until the day we die? This is why it's not just a "bad day" that will pass or a "terrible date" that can be easily excused. It's an everyday struggle from a certain point onward, feeling mostly dreadful until we find a way to adapt our lifestyles, seek HRT, or explore other solutions—because there are solutions.

Now, I'm not suggesting that every woman has to feel awful during this time. I understand that some women sail through menopause relatively unscathed, much like how some experienced severe premenstrual tension while others didn't. However, if our hormones control every aspect of our bodies, it's possible that some women's hormones don't fluctuate as wildly, or that our individual tolerance for change contributes to our differences.

As the latest research, long overdue, suggests, we need to maintain oestrogen levels to protect against heart disease, osteoporosis, and even dementia. If that's the case, should women routinely be tested at 50 to ensure they remain protected from these health issues, even if they feel fine? I believe the answer is yes.

I want to conclude this chapter on a positive note because, as with everything in life, there are silver linings and different perspectives to consider. Menopause brings an end to periods, liberating women from the nesting instinct that sometimes causes them to prioritise the needs of others over their own well-being. Your tolerance for certain people or situations decreases, and you gather the courage to make changes in friendship circles, relationships, and even embark on new careers or pursue exciting interests. We may mourn the loss of our childbearing capacity or, in my case, the boundless energy and drive of youth, but we gain far more than we lose. Even in the ritualistic sense of grieving and loss, as we approach and surpass 50, we mourn the woman we once were, fearing that she is forever lost. But with death comes rebirth.

We are reborn, stepping into the next phase of our lives, embracing our beautiful goddess forms, unshackled by societal expectations, people-pleasing, or anything that diminishes our true selves. I personally struggled with the prospect of turning 50, but something shifted within me and I embraced it. I looked around and marvelled at the awe-inspiring older female friends and mentors in my life, who possessed more knowledge, wisdom, experience, and grace than many could fathom. Vibrant, confident, accomplished, the sparkle in their eyes outshone any lines on their skin, accentuating the softness of their beautiful, well-lived features. I celebrate women—all women—but none more than those who graciously share their words of guidance, self-love, and acceptance with those of us who have been there, done that, and are soaring high in our own fabulousness, let's follow suit.

Please, do not fear the changes that await us all. Reach out to your fellow women for advice and support. Let us be assertive and direct in our requests for help from the medical profession, continuously demanding more from them. It is their duty to listen, learn, and assist you. Accept nothing less than what you deserve. You are that goddess—my goddess.

Decoded 7
Health

Chapter 7

QUAKONOMICS

Recently, one of my clients shared a disturbing health incident she had endured. During our skin consultation process, we meticulously discussed her medical history and lifestyle for over an hour to ensure that our treatments were suitable and safe. As we explored the illnesses she had experienced, this seemingly healthy and fit woman in her early forties confided in me about suffering a stroke a few years earlier. The circumstances surrounding her stroke remained speculative, as her overall health was excellent. However, it turned out that her personal trainer had been pushing her beyond her limits, subjecting her to intense workouts with heavy weights on her back without correcting her form. This irresponsible approach had compromised her blood supply, triggering a chain of events that led to the stroke. While this was an uncommon occurrence, what she shared next left me utterly astounded.

She described experiencing classic stroke symptoms: numbness on one side of her body, a pounding headache, and sudden pain and nausea.

Urgently seeking medical attention, she had a brief conversation with a doctor who swiftly dismissed her symptoms as a panic or anxiety attack. Despite adamantly insisting that she did not suffer from either condition and did not feel particularly stressed, she was sent home with patronising advice to relax and prescribed beta blockers.

However, a week later, she found herself back in the hospital, experiencing further symptoms that turned out to be the aftermath of the stroke. The doctor she saw on this occasion confirmed that she had indeed suffered a stroke a week earlier. She wasn't surprised, as she had known something was profoundly wrong and suspected a stroke.

What shocked me the most about this distressing example of flagrant misogyny was not just the patronising and belittling treatment she received, insinuating that this "silly girl" was wasting valuable hospital time, but also the fact that she didn't seem overly angry or disgusted by this potentially life-threatening and utterly negligent lack of care. Was she so indoctrinated into the prevailing myth that doctors are infallible and know what is best for us, attributing it to a rare mistake?

Furthermore, considering that the majority of doctors in the recent past tended to be male, does it imply that women are not as predisposed to the sciences as men, therefore making it inappropriate to question them?

The gravity of this situation and the disregard for her well-being due to blatant gender bias left me seething. It serves as a stark reminder that we still have a long way to go in dismantling such systemic injustices within our healthcare system.

This exchange further encouraged me to delve deeper into this topic. I couldn't help but reflect on the historical role of women as healers. Throughout time, it was women who possessed the knowledge, care, and nurturing qualities that naturally complemented the practice of medicine. So, when and why did men take over this domain, depriving those who possessed an innate sense of compassion, generations of inherited wisdom, and appropriate bedside manner?

Recalling similar anecdotes from the past, I was determined to explore further. That's when I stumbled upon an insightful book called *"Doing Harm" by Maya Dusenbury*. Finally, I found a substantial body of research shedding light on the matter. The book presented numerous examples of women being misdiagnosed, with compelling narratives that illustrated instances where women had been wrongly diagnosed. For instance, pericarditis, a condition deserving proper medical attention, had been hastily attributed to anxiety. In another case, a severe bacterial infection had been carelessly dismissed as mere stress. The list of such instances seemed endless.

While reading the book and coming across numerous examples of medical misdiagnoses, I was shocked by the alarming frequency of such incidents and the prevailing assumptions surrounding women's health. It reminded me of a personal experience I had with a male consultant, which thankfully wasn't life-threatening but still exposed me to this kind of treatment.

I visited a local private hospital seeking assistance for my problematic knees, which were affected by a birth defect causing slight misalignment of my kneecap. The consultant, an older gentleman, condescendingly advised me to "lose weight" and suggested I should "start going to the gym." He even went as far as explaining that he didn't mean to "do aerobics and then eat a Mars Bar," making wild assumptions about me after conversing for less than two minutes.

Ironically, at the time of this conversation, I had recently completed a half marathon and frequented the gym three times a week for spinning, Body Pump classes, and regular runs. My husband accompanied me to the appointment, and astonishingly, the consultant directed all his "helpful" remarks to my husband instead of me. I was dumbfounded, and in response, I managed to utter that I did, in fact, go to the gym. However, he simply looked past me, addressing my husband, who was equally appalled by witnessing such disrespectful treatment toward his wife. Without hesitation, we both stood up and left, having paid £250 for the pleasure of that condescending pep talk.

Although I found all the information in the book to be shocking, one particular revelation struck me the most—the lack of research on women in heart disease and other cardiovascular conditions. Most research in this field has been conducted on 75kg white men, with minimal focus on women. It's a disheartening reality that underscores the gender bias prevalent in medical research.

The book also provided insights into a question that had been on my mind for years: how and when did men take over the field of medicine, considering that "modern" medicine hasn't been around for that long in the grand scheme of things? The book primarily focuses on the United States, but it's worth noting the saying, "when the US sneezes, the UK gets a cold." The historical trajectory of medicine in the UK likely followed a similar path.

Until the late 18th century, healing was not a profession but more of a "neighbourly service," with knowledge passed down through generations and shared by native Americans about local herbs and their healing properties. It's important to remember that everything we need to cure ailments already exists on this planet; we just haven't discovered it all yet. Many women dedicated their lives to this form of healing, along with some men, often of native or ethnic descent.

Then came a new class of professional "doctors" who sought to commoditize healing. They resorted to extreme treatments like using arsenic and bloodletting to showcase their abilities, although these methods were neither sophisticated nor successful. This era was known as "heroic medicine," characterised by bleeding and purging methods.

Around the early 19th century, the systematic exclusion of women and anyone who wasn't wealthy and white began. To summarise a lengthy and fascinating story, men joined forces and implemented legislative barriers, shutting down medical schools that weren't approved by the newly formed American Medical Association (AMA). These self-proclaimed expert doctors, with the assistance of the Carnegie Foundation, ensured that only AMA-approved medical schools operated, perpetuating discrimination. This brings us to 1970, when only 10% of doctors were female. According to the book, a survey of admissions officers found that nineteen out of twenty-five American medical schools admitted to giving preference to male applicants unless a female applicant demonstrated superior qualifications.

In 1972, a landmark class-action lawsuit was filed against a medical school that no longer allowed gender discrimination. By the late 1970s, the number of female applicants had tripled. However, even in 1980, only 12% of obstetricians and gynaecologists were women.

As of 2023, the percentage has increased to 85% in the US. Although I don't have the exact numbers for the UK from the detailed history I learned from *Ms Dusenbury's* enlightening book. However it's safe to assume that the UK and US shared a similar trajectory in these matters. It becomes apparent that certain things have remained a certain way for so long that they are not questioned.

The book sheds light on the question of why men have dominated reproductive health and medicine. When we stop and consider this, it becomes clear that men knowing more about our reproductive health than women doesn't sound right. Are we brainwashed to accept this because it has always been this way? Is it acceptable that we put our health in the hands of men who have no concept of what it is to be a woman, and then we get treated as if we can't think for ourselves or know what's best for us?

Similar advice regarding women's health and weight loss in the UK remains woefully outdated. A client of mine, who is a couples counsellor, shared her experience. She had recently turned 50 and had started hormone replacement therapy (HRT) a year ago, which had significantly improved her well-being. During her 6-month check-up with the menopause nurse specialist at her GP's office (a positive development), despite her weight being lower than the previous year, the nurse advised her to join the NHS "Fat Club" based on her BMI, claiming she was very overweight. I was shocked because there was no way you would look at this lady and consider her just overweight, let alone "very" overweight. In fact, she had taken the initiative to educate herself about coping with menopause from various sources, improved her diet by cutting back on sugar and processed foods, reduced her alcohol consumption, and started walking more and doing half an hour of weights at home a few times a week. She was much healthier than the previous year. So why was she being told she needed help with her weight? The conclusion she drew was that it was because she had turned 50.

Interestingly, there is an important fact about the BMI scale. In the 1980s, when dieting became a profitable industry and pharmaceutical companies got involved, a couple of scientists were paid to "adjust" the BMI scale downward, making people feel fatter and creating a greater demand for diets. It was an early example of big pharma corruption that had nothing to do with improving the health and well-being of customers.

Throughout centuries and even millennia, women have traditionally cared for one another. We possessed the knowledge and skills to nurture fellow women through pregnancy and even handle childbirth ourselves. When we unite as sisters, we become a formidable force, as we have been throughout history. Reflecting on the past, we can observe that the local midwife in a village often possessed extensive knowledge and doubled as an herbalist. Alternatively, groups of women would come together to support and assist a woman during childbirth, ensuring her safety and well-being.

While it's important to acknowledge the advancements of modern medicine, there is a valid discussion to be had about the historical transition and its implications for women's autonomy in reproductive health matters.

You only have to look at *Roe versus Wade* in the US recently to see how the views of a handful of men can and will now cause massive suffering for millions of women by making abortion illegal in most states without exception, even for incest, rape, or other exceptional circumstances. They are even policing women who cross the border while pregnant for abortions. Regardless of your own feelings about abortion and as women, we may have mixed feelings about this, but I hold the deepest compassion for any woman who has faced the difficult decision of undergoing an abortion. While I personally have not experienced it myself, I recognise that my fortune in this regard is partly due to luck and my unwavering commitment to contraception since the onset of my sexual activity. I am acutely aware that not every woman shares the same circumstances or opportunities, and I believe in the importance of supporting and respecting the individual choices and experiences of all women when it comes to their reproductive health. The idea that this decision could fall to anyone other than the woman in question is simply abhorrent to me.

Speaking of contraception, this is an area where we could use a little more focus in terms of development from the companies that manufacture these products. In fact, I started taking the contraceptive pill at the age of 14 due to my horrendous periods and continued some form of contraception until I reached menopause.

When we consider puberty, as young women navigate the surge of hormones and grapple with the significant risk of pregnancy, many seek assistance in finding reliable contraception. Reflecting on my own experiences as a 14-year-old in search of solutions, it seemed that the options available were primarily the combined pill or condoms for those already sexually active. In my case, with heavy and irregular periods, the pill seemed to be the only viable choice. I went to my local family planning clinic, where they happily provided me with the pills I needed, and I was extremely grateful.

However, it is disconcerting that little progress has been made in terms of advancements in contraceptive medications. As I review the medical consent intake forms at my clinic, I am astonished to see the names of contraceptive pills that were prevalent during my youth still being prescribed to women today, four decades later. This raises questions about why women are still offered the exact same options without significant improvements, both in terms of limited alternatives and the next generation of hormonal contraception.

Moreover, if the medical industry fails to prioritise research on crucial aspects like women's cardiology, we cannot help but question the likelihood of sufficient investment in addressing women's health concerns such as contraception and menopause. These are issues that affect 50 percent of the population and demand comprehensive attention and exploration.

A recent conversation with a close friend highlighted a different perspective regarding her experience with the pill. It was very interesting. She had relied on it for the majority of her adult life until recently when she had to stop taking it due to an upcoming surgery. Finally, after years of being misdiagnosed, her struggles with endometriosis were being addressed after paying for private healthcare, a necessity to alleviate the immense suffering she endured for many years. To her astonishment, she discovered that her libido had soared. She had always considered herself somewhat indifferent and uninterested in sex, and as a married woman, sex had been more of a duty than a source of pleasure. However, she had not realised that the pill had been dampening her natural desires, and she and her husband of many years were enjoying this newfound connection.

It forces us to acknowledge the unfortunate reality that women's sexual pleasure is often dismissed and relegated to an afterthought, deemed unimportant in the context of contraceptive development. I must express my eternal gratitude to *Katharine McCormick* and *Margaret Sanger,* the pioneers behind the invention of the contraceptive pill in the 1950s. Their intentions were undoubtedly rooted in a desire to empower women and provide them with greater agency in matters of reproduction. The evolution of these discrete contraceptives has allowed women to take control of their bodies, bringing freedom to many of us. However, this also limits our options for voting with our feet or wallets when it comes to boycotting pharmaceutical companies and demanding more from the industry.

Now, let's shift our focus to the other side of reproductive health: childbirth. I recently saw a video of a hypnobirth on Instagram, featuring a woman having a peaceful water birth. It was a beautiful and wonderful experience to witness. The caption on the video asked, "Why don't we believe that all births can be like this?"

It's a stark contrast when we consider the sterile medical environment that women enter when they go to hospitals to give birth. They often face being talked down to or, even worse, being ignored and put in dangerous situations that they know in their hearts are wrong, but are belittled when they are most vulnerable.

Maternity wards are mostly understaffed, and it is often men who serve as doctors in these facilities, overseeing the process alongside midwives. There has been discussion about how many of these midwives suffer from internalised misogyny, blindly following orders that may contradict the principles of sisterhood.

Interestingly, my mother was a midwife, and I believe she genuinely cared for the women she looked after and everyone on her wards (she was actually the head of midwifery in her area). But those days of real, individual, mother-centric care seem to have vanished. It is rare for me to hear a positive birth story. When someone tells me they are pregnant and expecting their first child, I try my best to enthusiastically ask about their plans, but unfortunately, I am aware of too many horrible stories. These hospital birthing experiences have resulted in deeply traumatic births that have had long-lasting repercussions on the mental and physical health of both mother and/or baby, and I believe the majority of these situations could have been completely avoided.

Giving birth isn't necessarily a medical event; it is a life event. It should be a positive, wonderful, and almost magical time in a woman's life. Instead, it has become a medical procedure that is often unpleasant. The memories of the unpleasantness may fade due to the overwhelming joy of having a new baby, but this just cannot be right. In the same way that men control our actions, they have even taken over our reproductive systems.

I recently had a client tell me that her friend was set on having a home birth with no reasons against it in her mind. However, due to an unclear reason regarding the date based on the last day of her period, she was considered overdue and was told she had to come to the hospital to give birth. Despite her belief that her baby was not quite ready at that time and her repeated statements that she wanted to give birth at home, the powers that be reported her to Social Services for neglect of an unborn child. She was forced to give birth in a hospital, in an environment she did not want. It was an awful situation, with a woman being forced against her will to conform to the rules imposed upon her. Why should wanting to give birth in one's own home, in a relaxed, loving, and peaceful environment, be such an issue?

There is a noticeable reverence towards male doctors and consultants, particularly among female staff, which could explain why the medical profession tends to have the highest number of concealed mistakes. In recent years, we have seen many heartbreaking stories of utter negligence by surgeons and doctors being covered up by nursing staff and management.

One particularly cruel case is that of disgraced oncology surgeon *Ian Paterson,* who was responsible for butchering and disfiguring countless women. Most of these women did not even require a mastectomy as they did not have cancer. He operated with total impunity for many years, and the level of callous disregard he showed towards his patients was staggering.

His tribunal ruled that his actions were "serious, calculated, and sustained" over a 14-year period. He even told a woman that she had cancer, when he knew that she did not. As if that wasn't bad enough, he did this despite knowing that they were already at rock bottom both financially and mentally due to the fact that her husband was also undergoing treatment for advanced-stage cancer. He convinced her that paying privately for a mastectomy was her best chance of survival. Perhaps pure greed motivated him, as indicated by his lavish lifestyle with multiple homes and wine cellars, but it is likely that a power trip, a god complex, and his psychopathic, narcissistic personality were also factors. Thankfully, he received a 20-year sentence, but how did it take 14 years for him to be brought to justice?

A brave whistleblower, *Hemant Ingle, an NHS Consultant Breast Surgeon* who had worked with *Paterson,* noticed that something was not right when he read all of the notes. He discovered that *Paterson* was misdiagnosing fibroadenoma, a benign lump in the breast, as cancer, and he reported him to management in 2007. A report was commissioned in 2008 but was kept private, even though two other surgeons contributed to the report, raising major concerns (you can now find this information on Google, which is terrifying). Even when the whistleblower moved hospitals, he persisted and reported *Paterson* to another private hospital. Both the private and NHS hospitals' management were aware of what was going on, yet they did nothing. They knew for a fact that *Paterson* was subjecting female patients to unnecessary surgeries, removing their breasts when there was no sign of cancer. He even performed a completely unnecessary double mastectomy on a man. Only a few courageous individuals flagged his behaviour. *Paterson* even invented a surgical procedure that was completely ineffective and downright dangerous for mastectomies. Eventually, after many years and around 1000 known unnecessary procedures, the issue was finally addressed, and he was convicted. The NHS paid out £17.4 million to settle cases with over 270 patients who sued over unnecessary or botched surgery. *Spire Healthcare,* where *Paterson* worked, agreed to pay £27.2 million to compensate a further 750 patients, with 1500 more cases currently being investigated due to new information that has emerged.

I remember a motivational talk at one of our sales conferences many years ago, where we were taught about failure long before it became fashionable (think of the "fail fast" and other popular quotes you see on social media). We were always encouraged to retrospectively ask the main decision makers who awarded the tenders we bid for why we lost. Losing was particularly harmful for our pockets as salespeople, but perhaps equally damaging to our egos. However, we were advised to face failure head-on and learn from it in order to succeed in future deals.

The aviation industry was used as an example of a field that embraces a no-blame culture, which has contributed to its exceptional safety record. In the event of an incident or something going wrong on board an aeroplane, such as a near miss, pilots know that they can explain exactly what happened leading up to the event. They have the trusty black box, which keeps them honest and preserves the true information. This ensures that any issues are identified and usually fixed before disaster strikes. The safety record of aviation speaks for itself. It is still considered the safest mode of travel due to this culture of analysing mistakes openly and learning from them. The speaker shared a story about a new aeroplane model that had two near misses. The manufacturers were eager to understand what was going on, and upon investigation, they discovered that something as simple as the switch for the landing gear looked similar to the switch for the cockpit lights (the details might not be verbatim, but it was something similar in contrast). Because the culture of analysing mistakes was ingrained in the industry, the pilots felt confident enough to analyse their actions truthfully, which led to an immediate retrofit of existing models and a change in design for future models. That particular model has not experienced any issues since.

Now, imagine if there was a little black box in hospital operating theatres or in day-to-day hospital tests and diagnosis. Just think of how many lives could be saved! I am oversimplifying the issues in the medical profession, but it is safe to say that there is not a culture of openly or privately analysing mistakes. With consultants and surgeons often considered untouchable and rarely challenged, a corrupt, toxic, and ultimately dangerous environment is fostered. Just look at the case of *Ian Paterson*. And that's a case that came to light. I shudder to think about how many other surgeons are operating without accountability and with complete immunity.

Taking all of the above into consideration, we can begin to get a feel for the lack of due diligence in some medical establishments and in my research, certainly when it comes to women's health. It's no wonder that Hormone Replacement Therapy (HRT) has hardly improved since the previous generation. Again, I fear this apathy stems from the acceptance that women must suffer, that we will simply put up with it. However, if we stand together, moving in the same direction, we can push back against this thinking and relegate it to the dark ages where it belongs. Question everything, if something does not feel right or you are simply not sure, ask questions. Hold the medical establishment to account, do not just take a doctor's word for something. Get a second opinion, and make it clear you will research yourself. Do not be intimidated by qualifications or perceived 'status', no one is infallible and you deserve to be treated with respect and dignity at all times.

Decoded 8

Conclusion

Chapter 8

MIC DROP

Through writing this book, I've found myself delving deeper into my own identity and reflecting on the path I have travelled this far. With my two stepdaughters in mind, I contemplate the future landscape they will navigate in the years to come. I ponder the evolving nature of women's progress and yearn for unity in our shared journey. I question what will define a fulfilling life for them, how their relationships with chosen partners will unfold, and whether they will choose to have children. And if they do, will they find the support they need? Will women's healthcare advance and improve? As adults, our role is to guide our children to become capable individuals who question the world around them. I aspire for our children to be unapologetically bold, especially when society labels them as "difficult" for being assertive and independent thinkers. Moreover, I believe that the education system, particularly in the UK, is falling short in equipping our children with vital life skills. We must inspire our children, whether they are female or male to think for themselves, ignite change, and challenge outdated norms. We need the emergence of a new generation of intelligent and empathetic individuals who will assume leadership roles, shape their professions, and transform the workplace.

For women today, I encourage you to embrace love and compassion in your interactions with fellow females. While our life experiences and environments may differ, we all possess an extraordinary power within us. Women hold the key to life itself; we are divine, embodying the qualities of goddesses—love, light, and healing. We possess the ability to nurture while displaying unparalleled resilience. When we stand together, united in a shared cause, we wield the power to effect change. Transformation often begins with small steps, and it is my hope that this book sparks a questioning of the status quo, an exploration of alternatives, and the cultivation of personal happiness. By engaging in critical thinking and embracing mindful awareness, we can reclaim our autonomy and redefine our purpose. Through conscious choices, we hold the power to reshape the world around us, transcending the limitations imposed upon us. As women, we often serve as the cornerstone of our environments, influencing the lives of those around us. Let us embark on this journey together, empowering one another and creating a future where women thrive and the world thrives with us.

Thank you for reading.

I hope you thoroughly enjoyed this book and it has helped you in some way to decode your way to true happiness.

To spread the word **please leave a review** at the place you purchased the book so other women can also Decode Their Happiness!

I appreciate every single one of you.

Penny Dee

ACKNOWLEDGEMENTS

I dedicate this book to my beloved husband, Phil. Your unwavering belief in feminism and your love and consistent support have made my life easier in every way. Through your actions, you have shown me what true partnership, love and kindness mean by demonstrating that men can stand alongside women in the pursuit of equality and empowerment. Thank you for being a beacon of support and love and making me a nicer person.

And to all the men who stand beside us – our partners, fathers, sons, and friends – may you continue to embrace the principles of equality and advocate for the rights and aspirations of women. Your belief and your commitment to dismantling these unseen barriers contribute to a more equal and just society.

To my amazing publisher, Eloise Attenborough at Book Bubble Press for believing in me, you truly know how to bring out the best in me. Thank you for all of your support and long hours devoted to this book. I appreciate you so much.

May this book ignite conversations, challenge conventions, and foster a world where all women are heard, respected, and celebrated. Together, let us continue to strive for a future where every woman can embrace her power and shine her light upon the world.

With love and gratitude,

Penny Dee

BOOK INDEX

1. Derren Brown - Happy
2. Ruby Warrington - Women without Kids
3. Caliban and the Witch: Women, the Body and Primitive Accumulation
4. Julie Bindel - Feminism for Women
5. Vishen Lakhiani - The Code of the Extraordinary Mind
6. Dr James Fanu - Too Many Pills
7. Dr Carole Hooven - Testosterone
8. Maya Dusenbery - Doing Harm: The Truth About How Bad Medicine and Lazy Science Leave Women Dismissed, Misdiagnosed, and Sick

I have listed all of these books and other suggested reading on my website: www.pennydee.co.uk

INSPIRING CONVERSATION!

Dear Book Club Enthusiasts,

If you are searching for your next book club selection please consider KWEENS - Happiness Decoded.

I believe this captivating and thought-provoking book will stimulate empowering discussions, ignite diverse perspectives, and create an unforgettable reading experience for your group.

Why Choose KWEENS for Your Book Club?

1. Unveiling Women's Happiness: KWEENS delves into the fascinating realm of women's happiness, exploring its multifaceted nature and offering practical insights for achieving genuine fulfilment. The book sheds light on the societal influences, personal narratives, and empowering strategies that can contribute to a happier and more fulfilling life.

2. Shared Experiences and Empathy: Through compelling real-life stories, KWEENS captures the diverse experiences of women, creating a tapestry of relatable moments and shared challenges. Your book club members will

discover a sense of empathy and connection as they explore the universal quest for happiness and the unique paths each woman takes.

3. Personal Reflection and Self-Discovery: KWEENS encourages readers to embark on a journey of self-discovery. Thought-provoking questions and guided reflections invite your book club members to explore their own values, aspirations, and paths to happiness, fostering personal growth and transformation.

As the author of KWEENS, I am committed to supporting your book club experience. I am available for virtual author Q&A sessions or to provide additional resources and insights to enhance your discussions. Please feel free to reach out to me through my website or social media channels. **Embrace the Power of Connection!**

By choosing KWEENS for your book club, you will embark on a collective exploration of women's happiness, uncovering valuable insights, and fostering deeper connections amongst your members. Let the pages of this book ignite transformative conversations, inspire personal growth, and empower each member to cultivate their unique path to happiness.

Thank you for considering KWEENS as your book club reading material. I am confident it will serve as a catalyst for meaningful discussions and personal transformations within your group.

Wishing you enriching conversations and boundless happiness!

Penny Dee

ABOUT THE AUTHOR

Meet *Penny Dee,* a distinguished British author, award-winning business owner and motivational speaker.

Having gracefully transitioned from the corporate sales realm in her forties, she embarked on a remarkable journey of success, establishing thriving enterprises within the clinical sector. Beyond her professional endeavours. Penny finds fulfilment in her marriage, her commitment to rescuing elderly dogs, and her unwavering advocacy for women's rights.

FOLLOW ME

 @pennydeeofficial

 @pennydeeofficial

 @pennydeeauthor

 www.pennydee.co.uk

Penny Dee
Podcast

Sit back and listen as she puts her spin on life observations with a focus on happiness and the other topics covered in this book.

Scan the code to listen to the
Penny Dee Podcast.
On all major podcast platforms.

FREE BONUS

DECODE YOUR HAPPINESS
Workbook.

Continue your journey to Female
Empowerment!

Scan the QR Code to receive your FREE
Bonus Workbook.

Printed in Great Britain
by Amazon

25663469R00108